UPWARD!

Wesleyan Formation in Three Movements

Paul W. Chilcote

Steve Harper

UPWARD!

WESLEYAN FORMATION IN THREE MOVEMENTS

Nashville

UPWARD!
WESLEYAN FORMATION IN THREE MOVEMENTS

ISBN: 9781791029838

Library of Congress Control Number: 2023949414

MANUFACTURED IN THE UNITED STATES OF AMERICA

In memory of
Frank and Nellie Baker,
beloved mentors in living the Wesleyan way

– Contents –

– Preface –

John and Charles Wesley understood and practiced Christianity as "living faith." The phrase "faith working by love leading to holiness of heart and life" aptly summarizes their vision of the human response to God's call to serve the present age. They did not view the Christian religion primarily as a system of doctrine, despite the importance of theology in their minds. Neither did they view the way of Christ as a set of regulations to be followed. The words that stand out for them are words like *living, growing, loving, serving*. The Wesleyan way is a journey leading us ever upward in life.

Methodism does not hold a monopoly on this view; rather, this simply reflects the essence of the gospel. The Wesleys believed that Jesus came to give us abundant life (John 10:10). They yearned for this themselves and did all they could to share this gift with others. Moreover, they believed that the Spirit builds a fruitful life in each of us. This kind of abundant living emerges and grows as we abide in Christ and he in us (John 15).

The Wesleys wanted the early Methodists to live their faith, to enact their doctrines, and to behave their beliefs. Anything less than that is "dead orthodoxy," they said, a toxic Christianity that produces sour godliness—the devil's religion.[1] They vehemently opposed "traditionalism" (the dead faith of the living), but heartily embraced the "tradition" (the living faith of those sainted ones who have gone before). The

1. John Wesley, *Explanatory Notes upon the New Testament* (Bristol: William Pine, 1765), comment on 2 Peter 1:7.

Wesleyan way is a living way, and we have encountered so many people who are yearning for this kind of Christianity today. This way of living generates hope and love—the qualities which enable us to experience and advance the new awakening occurring in our time, a rediscovery of all people as God's beloved.

Unfortunately, some Christians today do not practice this Wesleyan way. The Wesleys described it quite simply as "primitive Christianity." We encounter Christians regularly who displace living faith with doctrinalism. They create never-ending litmus tests to determine who is "in" and who is "out." They over-emphasize doctrines that go far beyond the historic creeds of the church. They turn what the Wesleys called "opinions" into "essentials." This kind of legalistic view is far from the Wesleyan perspective we love. Even more importantly, it is far from what we know of Jesus's own life and teaching. He never asks about what we believe. His primary concern is how we love. The way of Jesus abandons power and control and excludes all forms of legalism, judgmentalism, and mean-spiritedness.

With this in mind, we are self-styled progressive Methodists, followers of Jesus committed to:

- a Christlike posture of humility that embraces all people and seeks to be transparent to God's love to every person every day through a spirit of invitation and openness;
- a winsome vision of redeemed life in Christ for individuals and communities, rooted in grace and advancing to the fullest possible love of God and all others;
- an understanding of theology as a means of grace for the world, leading to spiritual transformation and growth rather than spiritual certainty and doctrinal uniformity.

We believe that living the Wesleyan way is about love not law. We have no intention to drive a sharp wedge between law and grace, but we will always err in the direction of the law of love.

Together we have devoted nearly 100 years between us to the study and teaching of the Wesleyan tradition. For us, this has been life-giving. From books like *Recapturing the Wesleys' Vision* and *A Faith That Sings* to *Five Marks of a Methodist* and *Living in Love* we have sought to communicate the essence of the Wesleyan way. But we sense the need for a collaborative work that pulls some of our shared ideas and concerns together. Consequently, we are writing this book as an affirmation of faith that incarnates light, life, and love. We want to help all followers of Jesus move beyond polarization and dogmatism, and want to invite you into a path leading upward—a way of wisdom and wonder in and for the world.

We are writing this book against the backdrop of a belief held by many that we are living in a new awakening. Once again, God is doing a new thing (Isa 43:19). We believe the Wesleys lived faithfully in such a time and that they can help us live more graciously and lovingly today.

Paul W. Chilcote
Steve Harper
Feast of the Conversion of St. Paul, January 25, 2023

– Introduction –

The title of this book—*Upward*—communicates a couple of important ideas.

Upward implies movement. Early Christians viewed themselves quite simply as people devoted to a particular movement they called the Way. If you think about it, that is a rather strange self-description. What does this mean or imply? Well, first it implies that life is a pilgrimage. It is always on the move. Never static, this journey is always dynamic. It involves development and growth. The way is packed with meaning, purpose, and value. Movement also connotes a particular path. Faithful Christians in every age have followed in footsteps set out before them. Jesus said, "I am the way and the truth and the life" (John 14:6). To be engaged in this movement implies connection with Jesus, embracing a journey with Someone who says, "follow me" (Mark 1:17). Jesus offers an invitation—an open, honest, life-transforming invitation.

Upward implies progress. For the Wesleys, life moves towards a goal. Movement upward entails progress in a particular direction with a specific end in view. Think for a moment about that image of the Christian life given to us by the Apostle Paul. "The goal I pursue," he says, "is the prize of God's upward call in Christ Jesus" (Phil 3:14). Note his language—"the upward call." The Wesleys sought to live into the perfect love to which God called them. In many ways, the Collect for Purity from the Liturgy for Holy Communion of their beloved Book of Common Prayer defined their lives. "Almighty God, unto whom all hearts are open, all desires known, and from whom no secrets are hid; Cleanse the thoughts of our hearts by the inspiration of thy holy Spirit, that we may perfectly love thee, and worthily magnify thy holy Name, through Christ our Lord." Progress for Methodists means to love God with your whole being and to love others as fully as possible.

We believe that this Wesleyan vision—this upward movement toward deeper levels of love—is unique. There are many different Christian paths. You have many options before you as a follower of Jesus. Some of these alternatives are ancient, like the paths of Eastern Orthodoxy and Roman Catholicism. Others are newer in the long history of the Christian faith, like Protestantism and Neo-Pentecostalism. Each of these are subdivided into literally thousands of paths defined by particular emphases or doctrines or ways of worship or spiritual practices. We do not stand in judgment over any of these "other paths"; we simply bear witness to the fact that we find joy, peace, justice, and love in the Wesleyan way of living. We appreciate the open, engaged, and loving character of Methodism and feel that it has much to offer to the world.

Any tradition can be misrepresented or distorted. A living and dynamic movement can ossify into an inflexible, dry, and arid form of religion. John Wesley even spoke about this with regard to the movement of spiritual renewal that he and his brother founded. "I am not afraid that the people called Methodists should ever cease to exist either in Europe or America," he wrote in his *Thoughts Upon Methodism*. "But I am afraid, lest they should only exist as a dead sect, having the form of religion without the power."[2] He was concerned that Methodists would lose their first love—namely, the love of God and others—and fall into the trap of religiosity.

Likewise, the Wesleyan inheritance will always be open to interpretation. This is natural and to be expected. In our own time, in fact, Methodism is splintering into a number of alternative paths along the fault lines of biblical and cultural hermeneutics, and we grieve the way

2. John Wesley, "Thoughts upon Methodism," in *The Works of John Wesley, Volume 9, The Methodist Societies: History, Nature, and Design*, ed. Rupert E. Davies (Nashville: Abingdon Press, 1989), 527.

in which the term "Wesleyan" has been co-opted to represent perspectives that we find alien to the tradition. Another way to put this is to say that the divisions are being shaped by ways of being Christian that are not fundamentally Wesleyan.

The Wesleyan way that we have come to know and love is not literalistic in its approach to scripture; that feels more like resurgent fundamentalism. Methodists view the Bible as a dynamic, living document that draws us into God's love and shapes our living in our unique contexts. Our view of the Wesleyan heritage is not dogmatic in its theological orientation; that characteristic reflects a more Reformed way of doing theology. Methodists are "practical," not "confessional" theologians. From a Wesleyan perspective, the purpose of theology is eye-opening transformation, not blind conformity. The Wesleyan way is not congregationalist in its organization and structure; rather, it champions connection and unity-in-diversity in the Christian family. Some Methodists who claim the Wesleyan label as their exclusive possession have actually exchanged the spirit, vision, and orientation of the Wesleys, we believe, for other ways of approaching the Christian faith.

We need to be clear from the outset that we have no interest in participating in battles of any kind that end up destroying the practice of life in Christ. Most people do not live or want to live in this world of conflict and chaos. Our intention is not to pour fuel on this fire. In fact, we are rather tired of the wrangling, the acrimony, and the damage it does to the church and its mission in the world. We seek to write genuinely out of a heart of peace. This book is not an argument, therefore, it is a testimony. At a time such as this we feel compelled to bear witness, as Wesley scholars, in an invitational way, to what we believe is an authentic, winsome, and valuable living of the Wesleyan way. We believe that the dynamism, openness, and quest for unity-in-diversity that characterize this path have so much to offer, not only to Methodists, but to other Christians and even people who are sheep of a different fold (John 10:16).

As we have talked together about what we have learned about Methodism from our own studies of the Wesleyan heritage, several common themes began to emerge. These points of learning reflect the spirit, substance, and sphere of Methodism. We write about these insights in terms of the Wesleyan way of wisdom, the Wesleyan way of wonder, and the Wesleyan way in and for the world. These are not discrete areas of life or thought. They overlap or impinge upon one another at many points. Wesleyan theology is holistic, and we seek to model the kind of holism in which the whole is greater than the parts. We make no claim, therefore, that the insights we offer are unique. But when held together, we do believe they afford a winsome and liberating vision of life—a great adventure to be lived into the depths of God's love.

In this book we introduce you first to what we call the Wesleyan way of wisdom. We are using wisdom here in the sense of Isaiah's prophetic statement fulfilled in the person of Jesus: "The spirit of the Lord shall rest on him, the spirit of wisdom and understanding, the spirit of counsel and might, the spirit of knowledge and the fear of the Lord" (11:2). Note how many times Isaiah uses the term "spirit." That is what we are talking about here—a "spirit." The prophet contrasts the wisdom about which he is speaking with human wisdom which often overrates itself and disassociates itself from God. The key to wisdom is acknowledgment—an awareness and appreciation of our proper place in all our relationships and in the story of God's love in which we play our own part. In each of the three movements of this book, we engage you in four conversations around the respective themes. In this first movement on wisdom, we invite you into a dialogue about the platform of grace, the posture of humility, the practice of inclusivity, and the promise of love.

In Movement 2 we take a deep dive into the Wesleyan way of wonder. As we think about this path following Christ, we are often awestruck. There is something about it that elicits wonder in our hearts and minds, and inspires us to live wonder-full lives. Only poetry can fully capture the wonder of love in creation and redemption. John Wesley's translation of a Moravian hymn by Nikolaus von Zinzendorf puts these ideas into a language that truly soars:

> Ah Lord! Enlarge our scanty thought,
> To know the wonders thou hast wrought!

Unloose our stammering tongue, to tell
Thy love, immense, unsearchable![3]

We love to ponder the wonder in life and love. As we do this, we see the Wesleys' vision of reconciliation unfolding through creation, redemption, sustenance, and restoration. It is a theology of love enacted by the Trinity summarized as abundant living.

The final cluster of conversations revolves around living the Wesleyan way in and for the world. If the wisdom tradition of our faith shapes our spirit as Methodists, and if we express the Wesleyan substance of grace and love in our wonder at the universe of its Gods, then the "sphere" of living the Wesleyan way must be God's world. Where else do we live? Living in and for the world, therefore, defines our mission as the Wesleys' spiritual heirs.

John and Charles Wesley viewed the theological world in a profoundly contextual manner. In some ways, a bit ahead of their time perhaps, they had an intuitive understanding that all theology is by nature contextual. We have no place to live out our faith other than the context in which we are planted. Perhaps the Wesleys' sensitivity in this regard was due to the multiple contexts in which they found themselves throughout the course of their ministries. Unlike most people during their time, they were always on the move, engaging people wherever they found them. There was no such thing as waiting for anyone to come to them. Moving from a Methodist Society meeting among the desperately poor Kingswood miners to a gathering of obnoxiously rich detractors near the Royal Crescent in Bath necessitated shifts and adjustments that affected their theology and practice on all kinds of levels.

Not only was their theology contextual (meaning that they gave close attention to the cultural and social setting of their mission), it was also conjunctive. The Wesleyan both/and approach to practical

3. John and Charles Wesley, *Hymns and Sacred Poems* (London: Strahan, 1740), 75. Modernized text. All Charles Wesley hymn texts throughout this book are cited from the website of The Center for Studies in the Wesleyan Tradition, Duke Divinity School: http://divinity.duke.edu/initiatives-centers/cswt/wesley-texts or from other editions as noted.

theology provided a helpful methodology for engaging the world.[4] They conceived life in Christ as deep engagement in the world. While they were staggered, as most of us are today, but the monumental problems of their age, they worked tirelessly for shalom. This meant waging peace, fighting slavery, feeding the hungry, and trying to challenge systems instead of simply salving the wounds of injustice.

In this third movement, therefore, we seek to provide a guide to how we live in and for the world today. We want to follow the lead of the Wesleys in constructing a "practical theology" for today that works in real time with real people. This is where living the Wesleyan way really becomes living. The four conversations of this section explore gospel-bearing in a world parish, forming mystic-prophets for the world, honoring nonduality in everything, and living into the peaceable reign of Christ. Those are some power-packed phrases and we have had so much fun unpacking them in this movement filled with verbs.

We have described the three major divisions of this book as "movements" rather than sections or parts. Likewise, we call the twelve subdivisions of this book "conversations" instead of chapters. We use this unconventional language very intentionally because we want you to feel swept into the movemental nature of the Wesleyan way and into life-giving conversations. Early Methodism was a movement of renewal and we have no doubt that the community of faith needs this desperately today. We also feel that this language is invitational in nature.

We would love you to read this book with others. Nothing brings out depth of insight more than shared conversation on common questions and themes. Again, early Methodism revolved around the joys and discoveries of what John Wesley called "Christian conference." Confer with one another about these issues. Share your thoughts, insights, and feelings openly and honestly with each other. To this end, we have provided some questions at the close of each conversation in

4. See Paul W. Chilcote, *Recapturing the Wesleys' Vision: An Introduction to the Faith of John and Charles Wesley* (Downers Grove, IL: InterVarsity Press, 2004), which features eight critical conjunctions in the theology of both brothers.

an effort to help stimulate your dialogue with others or to reflect upon the reading on your own.

Methodists sing their faith while living it. Faith, in other words, puts a song on our lips as God's love rises from our hearts and draws us upward. Who better than Charles Wesley to provide some words of inspiration as we take our first steps together in our journey upward:

> Come let us arise,
> And press to the skies;
> The summons obey,
> My friends, my beloved, and hasten away!
> The Master of all
> For our service doth call,
> And deigns to approve
> With smiles of acceptance our labour of love.
>
> His burden who bear,
> We alone can declare
> How easy his yoke;
> While to love and good works we each other provoke,
> By word and by deed,
> The bodies in need,
> The souls to relieve,
> And freely as Jesus hath given to give.[5]

5. Charles Wesley, *Hymns and Sacred Poems,* 2 vols. (Bristol: Farley, 1749), 2:280.

MOVEMENT 1

The Way of Wisdom

– Introduction –

Methodists may not think immediately of their Wesleyan legacy as a way of wisdom. But we are convinced they should. Wisdom is different from knowledge. Simply knowing about something does not guarantee that you will use your knowledge wisely. Education, for example, is a great gift. But instead of using your education—your knowledge—for the benefit of others, you can easily turn it into a weapon against other people. Knowledge devoid of wisdom can be dangerous.

In the same way, someone can know a lot about Jesus, but that knowledge can be turned into an "I know and you don't" mentality. Knowledge, if mishandled, can foster arrogance and pride. It can nurture a sense of superiority in us that breeds contempt for those who don't know what we know or understand the truth as we do. Before you know it, the way you act is nothing like the Jesus you say you know. Unfortunately, we see a lot of this kind of behavior in the life of the church today. It grieves us deeply when those who claim to be the followers of Jesus exhibit this sense of superiority over others, self-righteousness, and most regrettably, the desire to win above all things. These attitudes and behaviors are antithetical to the Jesus we know. But this misunderstanding—this lack of wisdom—about how you live what you know is nothing new. This theme, in fact, pervades the Bible.

The Old Testament makes it abundantly clear that God chose the Hebrews as a special people. But it also demonstrates that God elected Israel for responsibility—to be a beacon of light and hope in the world. The people of Israel, however, exchanged their election to responsibility for a sense of special, even unrivalled, privilege. Instead of offering God's light and love freely to others, they lived as though "they were chosen and others were not." They lived as though they were on the top and others were on the bottom. Instead of being blessed to be a blessing to others, they interpreted their election as power, prestige, and privilege. They had knowledge—even deep knowledge about God—but they lacked wisdom. Prophets, therefore, had to call them back to God's original intention, to demonstrate God's greater wisdom. Indeed, Walter Brueggemann notes that wisdom is the maturation of the formative flow of Old Testament literature.[1]

This tragic saga about misunderstood election led eventually to the coming of Jesus into the world to demonstrate once-and-for-all the way of God. Rather than using his power against others, Jesus takes on the form of a servant and assumes ultimate responsibility for his brothers and sisters in the human family. He relinquishes his life in a mission of self-sacrificial love. Jesus demonstrated a wisdom few understood. His life looked like foolishness to those living by the standards of the world and not by God's spirit. But in his life, we see the wisdom of God's universe writ large.

Despite this, some of Jesus' followers perpetuated the old pattern of knowledge devoid of wisdom. Originally, some Jewish Christians, for example, looked down on Gentiles—those who lived and believed differently than they did. In order to overcome these restrictive and nationalistic tendencies, a council was held in Jerusalem to discuss these issues. The church leaders came to the conclusion that the "way of Jesus" was universal and should not be restricted to any particular people (Acts 15; Gal 2).

But this did not eradicate other exclusivist attitudes. Those who were free looked down on slaves. Leaders in many communities even excluded women from participating fully in the life of the church. Again, in an effort to eradicate these exclusivist attitudes and practices,

1. Walter Brueggemann, *Spirituality of the Psalms* (Minneapolis: Fortress Press, 2001). Wisdom literature communicates the reorientation/restoration motif in the Old Testament.

St. Paul issued an egalitarian manifesto second to none in the pages of the New Testament: "There is no longer Jew or Greek, there is no longer slave or free, there is no longer male and female; for all of you are one in Christ Jesus" (Gal 3:28). There were to be no winners and losers in the family of God. Wisdom prevailed. St. Paul wrote of the ongoing significance of this when he referred to Christ, in fact, as the wisdom of God (1 Cor 1:24).[2]

So what does wisdom look like for those who seek to understand and live their faith through a Wesleyan lens? We address this critical question in this first movement through four conversations.

- First, the way of wisdom is founded upon *the platform of grace*. The Wesleys oriented their whole vision of life in Christ around the concept of grace. Every aspect of their theology reflects some facet of God's grace, particularly as we find it embodied in Jesus.

- Second, the Wesleys emphasized the importance of a person's posture in life. How we position ourselves in relation to others demonstrates how we seek to imitate Christ. If we really want to follow Jesus, then we will assume *the posture of humility*.

- Third, one of the most important debates in our world today revolves around the issue of inclusivity. In the Gospels, time and time again, Jesus transforms exclusivists into people with a wide embrace. His own life bears witness to *the practice of inclusivity*.

- Fourth, *the promise of love*. John and Charles Wesley made a special point to draw an intimate connection between grace and love. Charles, the poet of "love divine," put the promise of love at the center of life in Christ.

---

2. See Cynthia Bourgeault, *The Wisdom Jesus: Transforming Heart and Mind—A New Perspective on Christ and His Message* (Boston: Shambhala, 2008), where she explores the theme of wisdom in relation to Christ.

We invite you, then, into these four important conversations about the way of wisdom.[3] Each theme strikes at the heart of what it means to be Wesleyan. Even more importantly, they point to the spiritual wisdom of Jesus. Methodists have inherited a legacy rooted in grace, humility, inclusivity, and love. Let's talk about these things together.

---

3. If the genre of biblical Wisdom is relatively new to you, we recommend Richard Clifford's book, *The Wisdom Literature* (Nashville: Abingdon Press, 1998).

Conversation 1

The Platform of Grace

Paul was talking with a friend of many years one day. While their paths diverged rather radically, they've still kept in touch. His friend would most certainly define himself as a "none." That term refers to those who are unaffiliated with any form of organized religion. Like many nones, he considers himself to be spiritual, but not religious. The conversation went something like this.

"I know we don't talk much about religion, but really," he launched in, "why would anyone want to be associated with anything going on in the church today?"

"Wow," I responded. "What brought this up?"

"I had two crazies accost me on the street the other day," he continued, "who harangued me about whether I was saved or not! They were so accusatory and judgmental. How in the world would they think anyone would buy what they were selling?"

"I get it. I really do," I said. "So sorry. You know, not all Christians are like that."

"Yeah, right," he retorted sarcastically. "They claim to follow Jesus, and while I really don't care, I know enough to say that they bore no resemblance to Jesus at all. No compassion. No understanding. No love. No grace."

No grace. That hits hard. This "none" had some expectation of what you should find in a follower of Jesus, but no one in his circle of life conformed to the image in his mind's eye. It seems as though

Christian authenticity is in short supply these days. The more things change, the more they stay the same. This lack of love and grace among Christians was the very issue that triggered the movement of spiritual renewal spearheaded by the Wesleys in eighteenth-century Britain.

Charles Wesley, like many today, also struggled to find "true religion" among the Christians of his own day. In a hymn entitled "Primitive Christianity," he provides an idealized portrait of the earliest followers of Jesus.[4] Note how he describes their common life:

With grace abundantly endued,
A pure, believing multitude;
They all were of one heart and soul,
And only love inspired the whole.

But he lamented the evasive nature of such a community in his own time.

Where shall I wander now to find
The successors they left behind?
The faithful, whom I seek in vain,
Are diminished from the sons of men.

Something had displaced authentic life in Christ and he diagnoses the fatal flaw:

You different sects, who all declare
Lo! Here is Christ, or Christ is there;
Your stronger proofs divinely give,
And show me where the Christians live.

Your claim, alas! You cannot prove,
You lack the genuine mark of love:
You only, Lord, your own can show,
For sure you have a church below.

4. Wesley, *Hymns and Sacred Poems* (1749), 2:333–36. Modernized text.

Christians lack the mark of love. That was the problem then and that is the problem now. Charles affirms that authentic Christian living in a loving community of faith exists somewhere. It is just so hard to find it among those who claim to follow Jesus. What is missing? Love and grace.

As we talk together about the movements in Wesleyan formation, therefore, we begin with the platform of grace. This is so critical. Everything in Wesleyan theology and practice revolves around grace. Platforms in the cyber world function in ways similar to grace in the Methodist theological world. A platform provides the organizing principle for the whole system. It contains all the components necessary for connectivity. It links all the various elements that coalesce and work together for the creation of meaning. Grace connects people to God, people to people, and people to the world. It provides the ultimate sense of meaning to life and all it entails. Grace is the Wesleys' orienting concern. A conversation about grace in Wesleyan terms entails at least four different elements: the grace revealed in Jesus Christ, the free and unbounded character of God's grace, grace in both creation and redemption, and the implications for living in and through grace.

First, *Jesus Christ reveals the grace of God*. John and Charles Wesley maintain that we encounter grace most fully in Jesus. The Prologue to John's Gospel provides a clue to the meaning and significance of grace in our lives: "And the Word became flesh and lived among us, and we have seen his glory, the glory as of a father's only son, full of grace and truth" (John 1:14). In the Wesleys' 1780 *Collection of Hymns*, the most significant and complete hymnal of the early Methodist people, there are more allusions to this single verse than any other Gospel text. Jesus incarnates grace. He puts flesh on the concept of grace. Eugene Peterson translates this text in a marvelous way in *The Message*. He talks about Jesus moving into the neighborhood and demonstrating God's generosity inside and out, God's true from start to finish.

The sermons of John and the hymns of Charles Wesley all focus on this gracious character of God extended to every person and throughout creation, all revealed in Jesus. They frequently collapse the phrase "full of grace and truth" into the simplified "full of grace." Reflecting poetically on this language, Charles provides one of the most profound images related to grace:

> O Jesu, full of pardoning grace,
> More full of grace than I of sin;
> Yet once again I seek thy face.
> Open thine arms and take me in.[5]

Grace means loving embrace. Acceptance and completeness. Healing and restoration. In the same hymn, Charles refers to grace as God's "kindest word" and associates it with the "arms of mercy."

The brothers almost always use the terms "grace" and "love" interchangeably. If God's essence or character is love, then grace is the way in which we experience that love in our lives. Wesleyan theology teaches an expansive understanding of love and grace that links theology and practice. Thoughts about God cannot be separated from actions in relation to God. God's gracious love holds everything together and gives meaning and purpose to all created things. Whenever the Wesley brothers use the phrase "fullness of grace," they consistently paint a portrait of a God who is only love, who desires the restoration of all, who seeks to lift up all people. "But thou, O Lord, art full of grace"; Charles sings, "Thy love can find a thousand ways."[6]

One of Charles's hymns, sometimes entitled "The Immensity of God's Love," celebrates this unity of grace and love in Jesus. It is, perhaps, his greatest hymn about God's grace:

> Infinite, unexhausted love!
> Jesus and love are one:
> If still to me thy mercies move,
> They are restrained to none.
>
> Thy sovereign grace to all extends,
> Immense and unconfined;
> From age to age it never ends;
> It reaches all mankind.

5. Wesley, *Hymns and Sacred Poems* (1749), 1:158.
6. Wesley, *Hymns and Sacred Poems* (1749), 1:186.

Throughout the world its breadth is known,
Wide as infinity;
So wide it never passed by one,
Or it had passed by me.[7]

This hymn provides the perfect segway to a second element of the Wesleyan conception of grace.

Second, *God's grace is free and unbounded.* In one of John Wesley's classic sermons entitled "Free Grace," he describes grace as God's free gift in all and for all.[8] His concept of God's free grace continues to stand as an antidote against all forms of Christian teaching that restrict God's love and grace in any way. God offers love to everyone everywhere. Whether God's beloved children realize it or not, that love already resides in their hearts and souls. The Wesleys preached tirelessly about the way in which the Holy Spirit always advocates "for us" and never "against us."

In late April 1739, right at the outset of the Wesleyan revival when John initially published his sermon, he appended to it his brother's poem on "Universal Redemption."[9] In this hymn Charles extolls the grace of God in no less than thirty-six stanzas. Essentially creating a lyrical paraphrase of John's sermon, Charles summarizes the central point in several terse lines: "The glory of thy boundless grace, / Thy universal love" and "Grace will I sing, through Jesu's name, / On everyone bestowed." In a much more famous hymn, "And Can It Be," properly entitled "Free Grace" like John's sermon, Charles celebrates this Wesleyan conviction even more succinctly: "So free, so infinite God's grace."[10] In addition to the free and universal nature of God's grace, two other Wesleyan convictions stand out: the relational character and the all-sufficiency of grace.

---

7. Wesley, *Hymns and Sacred Poems* (1749), 1:163. Modernized text.

8. See John Wesley, *The Works of John Wesley, Volume 3, Sermons III, 71-114*, ed. Albert C. Outler (Nashville: Abingdon Press, 1986), 542–63.

9. "Universal Redemption," in John Wesley, *Free Grace* (Bristol: Farley, 1739), 31–35. Modernized text.

10. John and Charles Wesley, *Hymns and Sacred Poems* (Bristol: Farley, 1739), 118.

Christians sometimes think about grace as if it were a thing. This idea was particularly commonplace in the medieval world when church leaders used this popular understanding to their political advantage. Grace equaled power, and they could wield that power to their own benefit. As a thing, grace could be given or withheld by those who controlled it. They could use grace as a weapon, and they did. The Wesleys moved sharply away from this view of grace as substance and shifted the category in a different direction. Instead, they understood grace in a relational way as God's unexplained lovingkindness. They proclaimed grace as God's offer of loving relationship to every person and God's meeting with every person at their point of need. Grace is nothing other than God's lavish, generous, unconditional love poured out on us, enveloping and wooing us into relationships of love. God expresses that love in different ways depending on where we are in this all-important relationship.[11] Regardless, God's grace is ever present relationally to enlighten, convict, pardon, reconcile, restore, and love.

The Wesleys also discovered the all-sufficiency of God's grace through their own relationships with and experience of God. The God they had come to know in Jesus Christ was a God of grace, mercy, and love. God's grace had changed their lives. It led to their own spiritual rebirth and generated their movement of renewal in the life of the church. Charles had been particularly influenced by Matthew Henry's vision, described so vividly in his biblical commentary: "The springs of mercy are always full, the streams of mercy always flowing. There is mercy enough in God, enough for all, enough for each, enough forever."[12] In his great hymn, "Jesu, Lover of My Soul," Charles proclaims of Jesus: "Thou art full of truth and grace. / Plenteous grace with thee is found."[13] Love equals grace; grace equals mercy. For the

---

11. While grace is essentially God's offer of relationship and restoration, the Wesleys describe it as prevenient, convincing, justifying, and sanctifying, in order to describe the way in which people experience God's extension of love at various points in the spiritual journey. We will explore all these aspects of grace in Movement 2 on the way of wonder.

12. Quoted in Wesley, *Works*, 7:383.

13. John and Charles Wesley, *Hymns and Sacred Poems* (London: Strahan, 1740), 68.

Wesleys, all this was visceral. Charles describes so well the deep desire the experience of grace evokes. "Keep me, keep me, gracious Lord," he sings, "And never let me go."[14]

Third, *the grace of both creation and redemption shape how we live.* To use a musical image, the Wesleys celebrate the grace of God in the song of creation and in the new song of redemption in Jesus Christ. Both of these melodies revolve around the keynote of grace. God's creation of all things out of nothing was God's first great act of grace. Our individual desires to make this song a solo, however, bring discord to God's song. Our own tones and rhythms disrupt and destroy the beauty that God intended. Through the grace of redemption God restores the original song of life. It is not so much that redemption stands over against creation; rather, Jesus sings the song of new creation in such a way that all can hear and join in. He unites the human family and all creation potentially by teaching us the melody and harmony of the original creation anew. This new song of grace engages all creation in one great act of praise.

Original creation reflects the dance of the Three-One God.[15] God's song leads all creation into the dance of journey, joy, justice, and jubilee. Given the fact that God is a nexus of relationships, relationship stands at the center of all life created in God's image. All these relationships necessarily entail companionship in a journey. God creates all things so that they may joyfully radiate God's love and participate in God's reign of peace with justice in the life of the world. Through the grace of new creation God seeks to repair or restore all aspects of the created order that have fallen out of sync with the overarching design of goodness, beauty, and love. Redemption anticipates the dance of jubilee in which all things are restored to God's loving purposes.

Charles Wesley plays with the biblical narrative of creation in an amazing hymn that celebrates the integrity of creation and redemption in the Wesleyan way:

---

14. John and Charles Wesley, *Hymns and Sacred Poems* (Bristol: Farley, 1742), 73–74.

15. We will explore this Trinitarian conception of God and its implications for living the Wesleyan way in Conversation 5 below on creation as an aspect of the way of wonder.

If drawn by thine alluring grace
    My want of living faith I feel,
Show me in Christ thy smiling face;
    What flesh and blood can ne'er reveal,
Thy coeternal Son display,
    And call my darkness into day.

The gift unspeakable impart:
    Command the light of faith to shine,
To shine in my dark, drooping heart,
    And fill me with the life divine;
Now bid the new creation be!
    O God, let there be faith in me![16]

In his sermon "On Working Out Our Own Salvation," John Wesley talks about two grand heads of doctrine upon which the Christian life is built.[17] The first is grace as it pertains to the work of God *for* us in Jesus Christ; the second is grace as it pertains to the work of God *in* us through the power of the Holy Spirit. Grace is God's unmerited love, restoring our relationship to God and renewing God's own image in our lives. Nothing was more critical to the Wesleys than this understanding of spiritual restoration founded upon God's unconditional love. Living the Wesleyan way is, first and foremost, a grace-filled response to God's all-sufficient grace.

Fourth, *moving upward implies a life of grace upon grace*. The practice of life in Christ begins in grace, grows in grace, and finds its ultimate completion in God's grace. To put this very simply, those who have experienced God's grace, live graciously. They become the instruments of God's unconditional love and grace to others. Others experience God's grace through you. According to the Wesleys, those who have embraced God's grace—God's offer of loving relationship—exhibit two distinguishing characteristics above all others: gratitude and benevolence. In his sermon on "The Unity of the Divine Being"

16. Charles Wesley, *Hymns for Those that Seek and Those that have Redemption in the Blood of Jesus Christ* (London: Strahan, 1747), 18–19.

17. See Wesley, *Works*, 3:199–209.

John describes true religion as "gratitude to our Creator and supreme Benefactor, and benevolence to our fellow-creatures. In other words, it is the loving God with all our heart, and our neighbour as ourselves."[18]

The word "gratitude" shares the same root as the word "grace," which basically means "thanksgiving." Grace and gratitude are all about an internal disposition of thankfulness. Those who live the Wesleyan way radiate this spirit of joyful thanks for life and love. If thanks is in your heart, other people see it. Charles Wesley captures this spirit of gratitude in one of his "family hymns":

> With singing we praise
> The original grace
> By our heavenly Father bestowed;
> Our being receive
> From his bounty, and live
> To the honour and glory of God.
>
> For thy glory we are,
> Created to share
> Both the nature and kingdom divine;
> Created again,
> That our souls may remain
> In time and eternity thine.[19]

God's grace and love in Christ elicit reciprocal love. For the Wesleys, our love of God move us to love our neighbor as well. In his sermon on "The Case of Reason Impartially Considered," John explains how love of neighbor—what he means by benevolence—springs from gratitude to God.

> As reason cannot produce the love of God, so neither can it produce the love of our neighbour, a calm, generous, disinterested benevolence to every child of man. This earnest, steady goodwill

18. John Wesley, *The Works of John Wesley, Volume 4, Sermons IV, 115–151*, ed. Albert C. Outler (Abingdon, 1987), 66–67.

19. Charles Wesley, *Hymns for the Use of Families* (Bristol: Pine, 1767), 175.

> to our fellow-creatures never flowed from any fountain but gratitude to our Creator. And if this be . . . the very essence of virtue, it follows that virtue can have no being unless it spring from the love of God.[20]

Elsewhere he proclaims: "And if any man truly love God he cannot but love his brother also. Gratitude to our Creator will surely produce benevolence to our fellow-creatures. If we love him, we cannot but love one another, as Christ loved us. We feel our souls enlarged in love toward every child of man."[21] Benevolence, for the Wesleys, includes all our efforts to partner with God to realize shalom in our life and world.

The way of wisdom begins with the platform of God's grace. All of us remain restless until we embrace the love and grace by which we have already been embraced. God's free gift of grace elicited the most amazing images and sublime expressions of gratitude among the early Methodist people. Hetty Roe, in a flight of spiritual ecstasy in a letter to her friend, exclaims:

> Great things, indeed, my dear sister, has the Lord done for you, and for your unworthy friend. And yet, O stupendous grace! we have only received a drop from the ocean of his love. An endless prospect, and a maze of bliss, lie yet before us! opening beauties, and such lengths, and breadths, and depths, and heights, as thought cannot reach or mind of man conceive! It is, my friend, the fulness of the triune God, in which we may bathe, and plunge, and sink, till lost and swallowed up in the ever-increasing, overflowing ocean of delights.[22]

---

20. John Wesley, *The Works of John Wesley, Volume 2, Sermons II, 34-70*, ed. Albert C. Outler (Nashville: Abingdon Press, 1985), 2:598.
21. Wesley, *Works*, 3:336.
22. Hester Ann Rogers, *An Account of the Experience of Hester Ann Rogers* (New York: Hunt & Eaton, 1893), 223.

Reflection Questions

Conversation 1 (Grace)

1. What part of this Conversation spoke most to you? Why is it important for you to hear this right now?

2. When and how have you experienced God's free and unbounded grace in your life?

3. Where do you see God's grace at work in the world, both to create and to redeem?

Conversation 2

The Posture of Humility

One of my seminary professors surprised those of us in a seminar he was teaching on Howard Thurman by bringing this larger-than-life spiritual giant to class one day.[1] We were all blown away when he walked through the door.

"Why don't we begin," our professor said, once our excitement had settled, "by letting our special guest say something about himself."

"Oh no," Thurman retorted. "I'd much rather learn something about each of these fine students. I'm more interested in knowing about them than in talking about myself."

"Well, okay then," our instructor responded. "Let's just go around the circle. Tell us your name, where you're from, and why you're in this class."

It was a small group, so we worked our way around the circle rather quickly.

"I just can't tell you what a joy it is to meet you all and to learn about what you're doing here," Thurman began. "I can tell you are all so sharp and ready to turn the world upside down, and the Lord knows, it could use that these days, and so could the church. Your professor asked me to reflect with you a little today, just from my heart, about truth. One of the main things I want to say is that truth has so much to do with your relationships in life. The posture you assume in

1. This was a seminar in which Paul participated, taught by Prof. Herbert O. Edwards at Duke Divinity School.

your relationships with others is going to shape your truth. My dear, dear friends—and I mean that—the ultimate test of your truth is the humility that it inspires."

When the class came to a close, Thurman said goodbye to each of us by name. We all felt, I am sure, that he really knew us and that we had made a friend. He is one of the most humble people I have ever met.

Moving upward means assuming a posture of humility in relation to others. The platform of grace leads us seamlessly to this insight. The spirit and wisdom of Methodism depend heavily on the quest for this virtue in life. Indeed, as all the great saints of the church have demonstrated, only humility provides an effective antidote to the disease of human pride—hubris. The Wesleys believed, therefore, that humility is the key to the Christian life. They learned this lesson most certainly through the influence of their parents. As young men they were both deeply influenced by the witness of great devotional writers like Thomas à Kempis who made humility the keynote of their vision of life in Christ. They took their ultimate clues from the life of Jesus—the self-emptying servant. God's invitation for us to assume the posture of humility speaks volumes about the nature of love.

First, *the virtue of humility must be cultivated.* Despite the two very strong personalities and wills of the Wesleys' parents, Samuel and Susanna, a deep sense of humility pervaded the Epworth rectory in which the boys were raised. Both parents were steeped in the Puritan tradition with its strong emphasis on humility and purity of heart. Evening reading in the home often found its way to these kinds of themes. The writings of John Worthington, one example among many, were favorites. An Anglican academic of the seventeenth century, he served as Master of Jesus College, Cambridge. One of his most famous books, *The Great Duty of Self-Resignation*, was published posthumously in 1675. Worthington discusses how humility predisposes our hearts to repentance, patience, gratitude, faith, and love. Humility is the virtue upon which all other virtues are built. The Wesley parents reminded their sons about the dangers of pride and encouraged them to cultivate humble hearts.

Second, *the imitation of Christ cultivates humility*. In 1654 Worthington translated and published Thomas à Kempis's *The Imitation of Christ* under the title *The Christian's Pattern*. John Wesley later published his own translation of this devotional classic, using that same title, and attests to the important role this devotional classic played in his own spiritual pilgrimage. In 1725, the year of his ordination as a deacon in the Church of England, he started reading *The Imitation of Christ* and "began to see that true religion was seated in the heart and that God's law extended to all our thoughts as well as words and actions."[2] In his *Plain Account of Christian Perfection*, Wesley quotes Thomas directly. He recalls his discovery that "'simplicity of intention and purity of affection' are the 'wings of the soul' without which she can never ascend to the mount of God."[3]

The theme of humility pervades à Kempis's spiritual manual for the Christian journey. At the very outset he links a biblical admonition to this central quality of authentic Christian discipleship: "True self-knowledge is the highest and most profitable discovery in life. Do not think of yourself, therefore, more highly than you ought and always think well and highly of others" (I.2).[4] Thomas counsels against anything that nurtures pride. Pride, he argues, creates an insurmountable barrier between ourselves and God and others. Moreover, since the sin of pride turns us away from our greatest good, we often need to be shocked out of our complacency and false sense of self-importance. Pride "defaces your soul," claims Thomas. "The humble enjoy continuous peace" (I.6).

According to Thomas, no force in the universe is stronger than an intimate relationship with the God of love which forms a spirit of humility in the believer. Love, not truth or knowledge, is the ultimate goal, and in this regard Thomas points consistently to the self-giving love of Jesus. He demonstrates how there is an intimate connection between grace, gratitude, thanksgiving (the topics of our previous conversation), and humility. Gratitude and humility, in fact, go hand

---

2. John Wesley, *The Works of John Wesley, Volume 18, Journals and Diaries I (1735-1738)*, ed. W. Reginald Ward and Richard P. Heitzenrater (Nashville: Abingdon Press, 1988), 243.

3. John Wesley, *A Plain Account of Christian Perfection*, ed. Paul W. Chilcote and Randy L. Maddox (Kansas City: Beacon Hill Press, 2015), 34.

4. Paul W. Chilcote, *The Imitation of Christ: Selections Annotated & Explained* (Woodstock, VT: SkyLight Paths, 2012), 5. All quotations from the *Imitation* are cited from this edition.

in hand. You cannot express gratitude to yourself! When you express gratitude to others, you are demonstrating that relationships define who you are. Humility is, ultimately, a relational concern. Humility is not an idea, it is a way of life—a posture.

Likewise, in his explorations of humility, Thomas connects this virtue closely with wisdom. Wisdom and humility do not simply happen; rather, you have to cultivate or habituate these dispositions. Your genuine appreciation for others, especially those who are different from you—and expression of wisdom—sows the seed of humility. Whereas pride nurtures hostility, humility cultivates gratitude. The only force potent enough to break down the barriers of human hostility is the power of divine humility. Thomas, and the Wesleys after him, believed that the imitation of Christ helps you learn how to do this.

We usually think of imitation in the sense of observing and replicating the behavior of some other person. Certainly, Thomas has this in mind as he describes humility in the life of those who truly seek God's will and way. On its most basic level, imitation of Christ means to live a Christlike life. But this means much more than simply mimicking Jesus. To use the image of St. Paul, it means "having the mind of Christ" (Phil 2:5)—cultivating a spirit like that of Jesus. While Thomas talks much about humility as an attitude or an attribute, he also stresses the fact that it is an action. He was a "practical mystic" who placed great emphasis on action, about not simply being humble but doing humility. He defines this virtue both as an attribute and an action. Humble actions that are Christlike flow out of a humble spirit like that of Jesus.

Third, *Jesus provides a profound example of humility as self-emptying.* Jesus assumed a posture of humility. He demonstrated the profoundly relational nature of humility through his actions. Humility functions as the primary building block of the Christian life. In his letter to the Philippians, St. Paul reminds the community to imitate the Christ of whom they sang in one of the earliest hymns of the church:

> Let the same mind be in you that was in Christ Jesus,
> who, though he was in the form of God,
> did not regard equality with God as something to be exploited,

but emptied himself, taking the form of a slave, being born in human likeness.
And being found in human form, he humbled himself
and became obedient to the point of death—even death on a cross.
Therefore God also highly exalted him and gave him the name
that is above every name, so that at the name of Jesus every knee should bend,
in heaven and on earth and under the earth, and every tongue should confess
that Jesus Christ is Lord, to the glory of God the Father (5-11).

This hymn of the early church combines the theme of humility with the act of self-emptying (*kenosis*). Jesus "emptied himself, taking the form of a slave"; he "humbled himself."

Charles Wesley's most profound exposition of this kenotic theme comes in a hymn exploring the titles of Christ. It is essentially a lyrical paraphrase of St. Paul's lyrical excerpt:

Equal with God, most high,
He laid his glory by:
He, the eternal God was born,
Man with men he deigned to appear,
Object of his creature's scorn,
Pleased a servant's form to wear.

He left his throne above
Emptied of all, but love:
Whom the heavens cannot contain
God vouchsafed a worm to appear,
Lord of glory, Son of man,
Poor, and vile, and abject here.[5]

These ideas of humility and self-emptying are distinct, but inseparable. In the incarnation God literally humbles God's self to the dust. Wesley provides here a portrait of a God who "laid his glory by." This God is the Eternal "contracted to a span." God stoops down and

5. Wesley, *Hymns and Sacred Poems* (1739), 165, 167. Modernized text.

condescends. God, in other words, comes down to the human level, enters into this world, and demonstrates the lengths to which love will go to establish and nurture relationships of love. The purpose of creation is to celebrate relationships of love. God seeks the restoration of this goal above all things. The essence of the paradox—the key to the mystery of love—is self-emptying. In his famous hymn entitled "Free Grace," referred to in the previous Conversation, Charles condenses the whole kenotic doctrine into that single line: "*Emptied himself of all but love.*"[6]

Fourth, *Jesus invites us to practice humility through actions.* In Jesus' life among his followers, he manifested this self-emptying love poignantly in the Upper Room. Here, among his closest friends, Jesus translates humility and self-emptying into a profound sign-act in his washing of the disciples' feet (John 13:1-20). Jesus acts out the meaning of God become human in Jesus and God's very purpose in creation. He demonstrates the paradoxical lesson that greatness in his community of the way is measured in terms of willingness to serve.[7] He asks for a towel and basin. He strips off his outer garments and begins to wash his disciples' feet, again taking on the form of a servant. He gives his followers an object lesson in humility that they will never forget. He provides a living image of discipleship—a concrete act of humility that defines the follower of Jesus.

He leaves no doubt, moreover, that he invites every child of God into the ministry of self-emptying love. In Charles Wesley's lyrical exposition of John 13, all of the kenotic themes converge into a compelling portrait of life in a self-emptied Lord whose example compels others into the path of humble service for others:

Jesu, by highest heavens adored,
The church's glorious Head;
With humble joy I call Thee, Lord,
And in Thy footsteps tread.

6. Wesley, *Hymns and Sacred Poems* (1739), 118; italics added.

7. See the treatment of the *diakonia* theme in Wesleyan theology in Paul W. Chilcote, *Recapturing the Wesleys' Vision: An Introduction to the Faith of John and Charles Wesley* (Downers Grove, IL: InterVarsity Press, 2004), 91–118.

Emptied of all Thy greatness here
While in the body seen,
Thou wouldst the least of all appear,
And minister to men.

At charity's almighty call
I lay my greatness by,
The least of saints, I wait on all,
The chief of sinners I.

Happy, if I their grief may cheer,
And mitigate their pain,
And wait upon the servants here,
'Till with the Lord I reign.[8]

The parable of the wedding banquet recorded in Luke 14 also provides a potent narrative illustration of the interconnected nature of humility and gratitude as well as humility and hospitality. Jesus tells this story when he notices guests beginning to jockey their way into positions of honor in the hall. "Go and sit down at the lowest place," he says, "so that when your host comes, he may say to you, 'Friend, move up higher;' then you will be honored in the presence of all who sit at the table with you. For all who exalt themselves will be humbled, and those who humble themselves will be exalted" (10-11).

The main theme of this great parable is joy—the sheer joy of being invited. God issues the invitation because of our need. We come to the table because we are hungry. All people hunger—all of us some of the time, and some of us all of the time. Those who have little testify to the indignity and pervasiveness of hunger. The rich starve inwardly, while appearing fat and satisfied on the outside. We hear echoes here of Mary's Song from the opening chapter of Luke's Gospel: "He has brought down the powerful from their thrones and lifted up the lowly; he has filled the hungry with good things and sent the rich away empty" (52-53). Understanding our human condition so well, God extends the invitation to all. In imitation of Christ, humble people relinquish

8. Wesley, *Hymns and Sacred Poems* (1749), 1:213–14.

the need to dominate others or to win. They don't wield their power against others. They don't weaponize truth or conceive certainty as the need to be right. Jesus promotes a vision of life in which we find peace and joy by elevating and serving others. We empty ourselves of power, prestige, and privilege and permit God's love to flow up to others.

Only humility possesses the power to conquer pride in the human spirit and make genuine love possible. Humility can only be sustained in those who put their whole trust and confidence in Christ, the One who did not think equality with God a thing to be grasped, but emptied himself of all but love. John Wesley reminds one of his early followers of this important reality: "This much is certain, they that love God with all their heart and all others as themselves are scripturally perfect. And surely such there are, otherwise the promise of God would be a mere mockery of human weakness. Hold this fast. But then remember, on the other hand, you have this treasure in an earthen vessel."[9] This acknowledgement keeps us honest. It reminds us that we need Jesus. It honors God's rightful place even as we affirm our place in the great narrative of God's mission in the world.

We really love the way in which Hannah Ball describes all this as a gracious process leading from total reliance on Christ to miraculous liberation into God's love. Humility leads to holiness, the fullest possible expression of love in our lives. Absorb the wisdom of her words:

> I want to feel deeper humility. I want humility enough to bear prosperity, and not to be high minded. I do not feel pride, but I wish to feel lowliness grounded in my heart. On examination, I find more self-contempt, more of the mind of Christ, and more of that love that suffers long and is kind.

> Thee let me now through faith behold,
> And by reflection shine,
> Till nature's dross is turned to gold,
> And I am all divine.

9. John Wesley, *The Letters of the Rev. John Wesley, A.M.*, 8 vols., ed. John Telford (London: Epworth Press, 1931), 4:208. Letter of April 7, 1763 to Miss March.

> Happy in the love of Jesus, I long to be with Him my soul loves. My heart is disengaged and free.[10]

Humility establishes true liberty. It includes freedom from our desire to be more or less than we really are. It affirms the genuine you in relation to all others as equals, as siblings, and beloved children of God. Humility finds fulfilment in the simple acknowledgement that you are God's beloved.

John Wesley traces the deep connections between humility and love as well in his *Plain Account of Christian Perfection*. "There is no love of God without patience, and no patience without *lowliness* and sweetness of spirit," he observes. "*Humility* and patience are the surest proofs of the increase of love. Humility alone unites patience with love."[11] Mary Hanson, an early Methodist woman, turned all these profound insights into a prayer. We invite you to make it your own:

> O, blessed fountain of love! Fill my heart more with [Thy] Divine principle. Sink me lower in the depths of humility, and let me sit at the feet of Jesus, and learn of Him. Enlarge my soul, that I may better contemplate Thy glory. And may I prove myself Thy child, by bearing a resemblance to Thee, my heavenly Father![12]

---

10. Joseph Cole, ed., *Memorials of Hannah Ball*, 3rd ed. (London: Wesleyan Conference Office,1880), 98.

11. Wesley, *Plain Account*, 148.

12. Quoted in Adam Clarke, *Memoirs of the Late Eminent Mrs. Mary Cooper, of London*, new ed. (Halifax: William Nicholson and Sons, post-1822), 170–71.

Reflection Questions

Conversation 2 (Humility)

1. What part of this Conversation spoke most to you? Why is it important for you to hear this right now?

2. In what ways do you seek to "imitate Christ" in your life of faith?

3. If you were to assume the posture of humility in your home, at work, or in your community of faith, what would this actually look like?

Conversation 3

The Practice of Inclusivity

In the very first episode of her blog, Inclusion Dialogue, Joanne Banks interviews Julie Allen, a professor of equity and inclusion at Birmingham University in the UK.[1] Joanna begins the conversation with the question:

"How did you end up working in the areas of equity and inclusion?"

"I was struck by the power of children's voices," Julie said. "After hearing what children thought about inclusive education, I decided that was the way my career was going to go. I still believe to this day that children and young people have the secret about how we should be doing this."

"When you heard young people's voices," asked Joanne, "what were they saying?"

"I heard that the young people were actively seeking inclusion," she observed, "and they were resisting the attempts to label them. They were quite funny about the teachers' lack of understanding about what it took for them to be included. They were informing me about being less up-tight about difference and just get on with all children."

"What do you think is required to get teachers to relax a bit?" Joanne asked.

---

1. "Interview of Julie Allen," Inclusion Dialogue, Joanne Banks; https://audioboom.com/posts/7734420-interview-with-professor-julie-allan, accessed December 23, 2022.

"I think they need to learn about difference and diversity as interesting and potentially a resource," she said. "They don't have to be frightened."

Concern about inclusion in all areas of life fills the air today. There are so many voices from the margins that speak wisdom into our world about the importance of diversity as a gift. Often those excluded or sidelined have the most important words for us to hear, if we have ears to hear their stories. Dr. Martin Luther King, Jr. coined the term "beloved community" to describe the heart of the Christian gospel. Jesus provided glimpses into this world of unity-in-diversity. He lived it daily. The rediscovery of hospitality, inclusivity, and what we like to describe as "the wide embrace," fuels a powerful awakening in our world today.

The practice of inclusivity looms large in the story of the people called Methodists. In this conversation we want to talk with you about this Wesleyan theme in two specific ways. First, we introduce the central role that spiritual practices have played in our heritage. Put very simply, we become what we practice. Second, we explore a particular practice of tremendous significance for our own time: the fullest possible inclusion of all people in the family of God. The Methodist movement was anti-exclusivist. The Wesleys intentionally included those often excluded from the community of faith in their own time and context. If we practice hospitality and inclusivity, the church begins to model God's beloved community to the world.

Practices shape our lives. Actions speak louder than words. One of the most exciting aspects of the time in which we live is the rediscovery of Christian practices and a renewed understanding of their purpose. Spiritual disciplines create openings in our lives where the grace, mercy, and presence of God may be experienced. These practices are means of grace—safe spaces in which our loving God embraces us. Practices defined early Methodism. John Wesley laid out a "rule of life" for the early

Methodist people.[2] He never viewed rules and regulations as instruments of control; rather, he conceived spiritual disciplines as instruments of liberation and empowerment. As in all other areas of Wesleyan theology, grace pervades these practices. Ultimately, those practices in which they engaged became ways of wisdom through which Methodists participated in God's work of love, grace, and shalom in the world.

John and Charles Wesley invited their followers to engage with them in the "practice of making room for all." Think about this as a critical Wesleyan practice that fueled the Methodist movement. Was this a work of piety or a work of mercy? Yes. It was both. To make room for others entails some serious interior work. It involves making space in your heart for those who may be different from you. It means asking God to change your attitudes. It also involves exterior actions—opening your arms to those around you and offering compassion to those in need. It means asking God to teach you how to create safe space for those who are outside, inviting them into the inner circle of your love.

Because of the emphasis on inclusivity in our beginnings, a "wide embrace" has always characterized our tradition. The Wesleys most certainly exercised a "preferential option for the poor," with many people from the margins finding a home in the Methodist Societies. The Wesleys made room for all sorts of people in their burgeoning movement. There was room for all: rich and poor, educated and illiterate, women and men, black, indigenous, people of color and Anglo.[3] Each generation of Methodists has taught this practice to the next generation. It is not too much to say that "making room for all" is in our nature.

But the Wesleys also connected inclusivity with the quest for holiness—the central theme of the Methodist movement. This pursuit begins in baptism with this critical question: "Do you confess Jesus

---

2. For some thoughtful reflection on John Wesley's use of a "rule of life" and how you might formulate your own rule, see Ian Bell, "Writing a Rule of Life," Exploring Devotion, The Methodist Church, https://www.methodist.org.uk/media/5035/dd-explore-devotion-writing-a-rule-of-life-0313.pdf (methodist.org.uk); accessed December 26, 2022.

3. See Leslie F. Church, *More About the Early Methodist People* (London: Epworth Press, 1949).

Christ as your Savior, put your whole trust in his grace, and promise to serve him as your Lord, in union with the church which Christ has opened to people of all ages, nations, and races?"[4] This understanding of who we are as God's people characterizes our pilgrimage from beginning to end. In fact, John and Charles Wesley considered inclusive attitudes and actions to be essential elements of holiness. For them holiness means inclusive love—love of God and love of neighbor (all creation).[5] If holiness entails conformity to the law in any sense, it is conformity to the law of love.

Likewise, at the table of the Lord we see this practice of making room dramatically enacted in the worshiping community. In Eucharist we live the parable of inclusion. We say, through our actions, that we want every person to know in the very depths of their being that they are welcome. One of Jesus' most consistent practices was eating with new friends in new ways, sharing food especially with those who were excluded. "Come to the Supper come," sang Charles, "*Every soul may be his guest.*"[6] The parable of the great banquet (Luke 14:15-24) serves as a paradigm of inclusion for him.[7] In a lyrical paraphrase of this story he sounds a note of urgency concerning the ultimate victory of God's inclusive love. In the peaceable reign of Christ, God invites all to the table. God offers grace to every soul. God excludes none from the offer of life in the reign of shalom to come.[8] As we engage in the Wesleyan practice of making room for all and celebrate around the table, we capture a glimpse of God's beloved community in which all are welcomed and all are loved.

The practice of inclusivity in Wesleyan formation includes at least

---

4. *The United Methodist Hymnal* (Nashville: The United Methodist Publishing House, 1989), 34.

5. See Paul W. Chilcote, "'All the Image of Thy Love': Charles Wesley's Vision of the One Thing Needful," *Proceedings of The Charles Wesley Society 18* (2014): 21–40.

6. John and Charles Wesley, *Hymns on the Lord's Supper* (Bristol: Farley, 1745), 7. Italics added.

7. See Wesley, *Redemption Hymns*, 63–66, where Charles proclaims to all people, "In Christ an hearty welcome find."

8. See Paul W. Chilcote, "Charles Wesley and the Peaceable Reign of Christ," in *Holiness: An International Journal of Wesleyan Theology*, forthcoming.

four particular elements that shape our lives in deep ways: the story of Jesus, the idea of wide embrace, the nature of hospitality, and the affirmation of the "other."

First, *we encounter inclusivity in the story of Jesus*. There are literally so many texts from both testaments of the Bible that we could marshal to make an argument for the inclusive nature of God's vision for the human community and the world. This great theme runs through the entirety of the biblical narrative.[9] The testimony of scripture, in fact, points to an "all inclusive" vision of life throughout the created order. The Bible celebrates inclusivity from the story of creation, in which we see God's delight in diversity, to the consummation of all things, in which "a great multitude that no one could number, from every nation, from all tribes and peoples and languages" worships before the Lord (Rev 7:9). It should be no surprise, then, that the Gospel accounts of Jesus—who came to proclaim and live out God's vision—are filled with images of mind-boggling anti-exclusivity and radical inclusivity.

When Jesus selects the twelve apostles, he includes men from every walk of life. They were unbelievably diverse. At the time of Jesus and in his cultural context, children, Gentiles, and women were viewed as either worthless or unclean. In response to the efforts of his disciples to exclude children from his ministry, an indignant Jesus embraces them (Mark 10:13-16). Jesus welcomes Gentiles, like the Roman centurion, into his community of followers (Matt 8:5-13). He recognizes a Canaanite woman's wisdom and insight, describing her faith as greater than that of his fellow Jews (Matt 15:21-28). All four Gospels demonstrate Jesus' willingness to go out of his way to embrace social outcasts and outsiders and welcome them into his new community of love. His words and actions universally demonstrate his opposition to exclusivity.

Out of all these anti-exclusivist stories, one stands out above all others, the story of Jesus' encounter with the Samaritan woman at

---

9. See Frank A. Spina, *The Faith of the Outsider: Exclusion and Inclusion in the Biblical Story* (Grand Rapids: Wm. B. Eerdmans, 2005) and Brandon J. Robertson, *The Gospel of Inclusion: A Christian Case for LGBT+ Inclusion in the Church*, rev. ed. (Eugene, OR: Cascade Books, 2022).

Jacob's well in Sychar (John 4:1-42). Take a moment and read this narrative in its entirety. This story paints the most compelling portrait of an inclusivist Jesus. Jews hated Samaritans because of their "racial impurity." They were half breeds—a mixture of Jew and Gentile. When Jesus encounters this woman at Jacob's well, she already has one strike against her. She is a Samaritan, unclean from the cradle. She is a woman. Strike two. For whatever reasons, she does not feel respected by the other women of her own community, waiting perhaps for the time she can be certain no one else will be at the well. Strike three. She is an outcast. When Jesus encounters this Samaritan female outcast, what does he do? He engages in the lengthiest conversation he has with anyone recorded in the Gospels.

In the wrong time and the wrong place, he extends the offer of relationship across the chasm created by culture and religion. But first, rather than engaging this woman from a position of power or strength, he approaches her in his need and weakness, permitting her to be the provider, the giver. He listens before he speaks, receives before he gives, and then offers life. The encounter proves to be transformative for the woman who then hurries home to share the good news that she has heard and seen in the Christ. This story perfectly illustrates how Jesus goes out of his way to include those who have been excluded. He offers them the gift of grace—a relationship of deep love that liberates and redeems. He welcomes despised outcasts into a new community of love in which they can both serve and flourish.

Second, *we experience inclusivity through embrace*. In his award-winning book, *Exclusion and Embrace*, Miroslav Volf explores contemporary concerns related to identity, otherness, and reconciliation.[10] A Croatian by birth, with firsthand experience of the attempted "ethnic cleansing" in former Yugoslavia, he considers xenophobia to be the most disturbing reality of our time. The concept of embrace, he believes, provides a most promising response to the problem of exclusion. The simple anatomy of an embrace—consisting

10. See Miroslav Volf, *Exclusion and Embrace: A Theological Exploration of Identity, Otherness, and Reconciliation*, rev. and updated ed. (Nashville: Abingdon Press, 2019), esp. 97–172.

of four basic elements—teaches important lessons about the nature of inclusivity. First, opening your arms communicates that you are not content to be alone. Second, waiting sends the signal that you do not want to impose yourself on anyone else. Third, closing your arms leads to an amazing paradox. You are being held and you are holding the other. Fourth, opening your arms again culminates the embrace. Neither of you lose your unique identity in an embrace, but you carry the other with you beyond that moment. The gift of the embrace encourages, empowers, and renews.

Our study of the Wesleys and the Methodist heritage has taught us two invaluable lessons about inclusivity and embrace. First, your own wide embrace will change you. You never know, in fact, how much your arms opened wide to another human being will change you. Moreover, communities of faith that extend a wide embrace change as well. Second, your own wide embrace will change others. You never know how much your empathy and offer of hospitality will change the "other." You never know how these powerful sign-acts of love will change the lives of those who witness them. Embracing others changes us. The gift of empathy changes others. The opening of the arms begins with the opening of the heart. Charles Wesley celebrates this quality in the life of an early Methodist woman, providing a lyrical portrait of the inclusive spirit:

> Celestial charity expands
> The heart to all the ransomed race;
> Though knit to [Christ] in closest bands,
> Her soul doth every soul embrace.
> She no unkind exception makes,
> A childlike follower of her God;
> The world into her heart she takes,
> The purchase dear of Jesu's blood.[11]

Life and love call us to extend our embrace, to wrap our arms around those we love and those we may not love so much. Our experience has

11. Charles Wesley, MS Funeral Hymns (1756–87), 45. "On the Death of Mrs. Hannah Dewal."

taught us that we actually do not know who we are until we embrace in this way. That embrace defines us just as much as anything else does—our personal belief, our doctrine, our worship. Christ calls us all to life not unlike his own: profoundly incarnational, tactile, flesh and bones, oriented toward an embrace. Embrace and hospitality go arm in arm.

Third, *we practice inclusivity through hospitality*. The writings of Henri Nouwen have always reminded us of John Wesley's approach to these very issues and practices. In his classic book, *Reaching Out*, Nouwen describes three movements as foundational to the Christian life.[12] We particularly appreciate the ways in which he plays with words. He talks, for example, about the movement from *hostis* (the word for stranger or enemy) to *hospes* (the term for guest or friend). He acknowledges the necessity of creating spaces, not of hostility, but of hospitality. In our Wesleyan heritage, conference, holy conversation, and hospitality are all part and parcel of our efforts to create connection and to experience God's presence in the midst of our journey in community through life.

Christine Pohl, in her study of the practice of hospitality, *Making Room*, describes the significance of Matthew 25 in our Wesleyan approach to this practice:

> This has been the most important passage for the entire tradition on Christian hospitality. "I was a stranger and you welcomed me" resounds throughout the ancient texts, and contemporary practitioners of hospitality refer to this text more often than to any other passage. Acts of welcoming the stranger, or leaving someone outside cold and hungry, take on intensely heightened significance when it is Jesus himself who experiences the consequences of our ministry or the lack of it.[13]

As others have observed, she notes that the most remarkable passage related to hospitality in the New Testament comes from the Epistle to the Hebrews. "Let mutual affection continue. Do not neglect to show

---

12. See Henri Nouwen, *Reaching Out: The Three Movements of the Spiritual Life* (New York: Image Books, 1986), esp. 63–109.

13. Christine D. Pohl, *Making Room: Recovering Hospitality as a Christian Tradition* (Grand Rapids: Wm. B. Eerdmans, 1999), 22.

hospitality to strangers, for by doing that some have entertained angels without knowing it" (13:1-2). A spirit of inclusivity provokes works of hospitality.

Fourth, *we promote inclusivity by affirming the "other."* Dietrich Bonhoeffer, the great Lutheran martyr of World War II, said that the church, if it is to be true to itself, must be a "church for others."[14] And this is exactly how the Wesleys felt about it too. The church does not exist for itself. It is not about you or me, or the local parish we call home. We exist to demonstrate God's love to and for others—to and for all. That is our reason for being.

In our own time, that word "other" has come to mean more than ever before. One of the most dramatic forms of exclusion in the life of the church today (alongside racism) has to do with the marginalization of LGBTQ+ kin. The harm perpetrated against beloved siblings in the name of Christ demands our attention for the sake of Jesus' way. While it is not possible to provide a thorough examination of biblical texts, concerns, and arguments here, we want to use this issue to illustrate the importance of living the inclusive Wesleyan way.[15] On the basis of the general tenor of scripture and Wesleyan spiritual values, three things have become immediately apparent to us with regard to our LGBTQ+ siblings. (1) They are beloved of God; love is their reason for being. (2) Their loving relationships can be expressed in sacredness, fidelity, permanency, and monogamy. (3) As beloved children of God they are invited to use their gifts to the fullest extent possible in the embodiment of God's vision of shalom.[16]

One final point on LGBTQ+ inclusion with regard specifically to ministry in the life of the church. Originally, John Wesley opposed women preachers. When several emerged in the life of the Methodist

---

14. Dietrich Bonhoeffer, *Letter and Papers from Prison* (New York: Touchstone, 1997), 362.

15. For a more thorough treatment of LGBTQ+ issues in the church, see Steve Harper, *Holy Love: A Biblical Theology of Human Sexuality* (Nashville: Abingdon Press, 2019).

16. See Paul W. Chilcote, *Active Faith: Resisting 4 Dangerous Ideologies with the Wesleyan Way* (Nashville: Abingdon Press, 2019), 14.

movement, however, this forced Wesley to re-examine the so-called prohibitive texts in scripture with new eyes. These statements were completely out of sync with his experience of the ministry of these women. He came to believe God called the women as well as lay men into this vocation. In the end, he welcomed women's ministry and became one of the women preachers' strongest proponents. Moreover, he made sure that those within Methodism honored those whom God had called. If God has called our LGBTQ+ siblings to this work and they display the gifts, grace, and fruit required for this ministry, who are we to stand in their way!

Wesleyan theology and practice provide the foundation for an anti-exclusive and radically inclusive way of living—a way of wisdom. Jesus modeled this way for us. He stretched out his arms of love on the hard wood of the cross so that all people might come within the reach of his saving embrace. Methodists make room for all because Jesus did. It is that simple. For the Wesleys, being ambassadors of reconciliation means reaching out, welcoming, and embracing. The practice and promotion of inclusivity creates a space in which God's beloved community can flourish.

Reflection Questions

Conversation 3 (Inclusivity)

1. What part of this Conversation spoke most to you? Why is it important for you to hear this right now?

2. What barriers stand in the way of you being a person of wide embrace? What can you do with God's help to break down the barriers of separation?

3. How are you actively reaching out to those who are different from you with love?

Conversation 4

The Promise of Love

Most of the conversations we have in life are extemporaneous and unscripted—off the cuff. Others, however, especially sacred conversations in community, take on a more formal quality. They are scripted, choreographed, even formulaic, shaped by centuries of rehearsal and performance. They are conversations nonetheless, and these conversations carry great weight. Excerpts from the dialogue of the baptismal liturgy reflect this quality:

Pastor: Do you, as Christ's body, the Church, reaffirm both your rejection of sin and your commitment to Christ?
People: We do.
Pastor: Will you nurture one another in the Christian faith and life and include these persons now before you in your care?
People: With God's help we will proclaim the good news and live according to the example of Christ. We will surround these persons with a community of love and forgiveness, that they may grow in their trust of God, and be found faithful in their service to others. We will pray for them, that they may be true disciples who walk in the way that leads to life.[1]

Here is another example of this kind of conversation, taken again from the worshiping community. It has to do with one of the most

1. *United Methodist Hymnal*, 35.

sacred moments in the lives of two people, their families, and the church. Like the conversation above, it also includes words of promise spoken in a context of great love.

> Pastor: Do you who represent their families rejoice in their union and pray God's blessing upon them?
>
> Families: We do. We love both of you. We bless your marriage. Together we will be a family.
>
> Pastor: Will all of you, by God's grace, do everything in your power to uphold and care for these two persons in their marriage?
>
> People: We will.
>
> Pastor: The Lord be with you.
>
> People: And also with you.
>
> Pastor: Let us pray. God of all peoples, you are the true light illumining everyone. You show us the way, the truth, and the life. You love us even when we are disobedient. You sustain us with your Holy Spirit. We rejoice in your life in the midst of our lives. We praise you for your presence with us, and especially in this act of solemn covenant; through Jesus Christ our Lord. Amen.[2]

These two conversations include promise-making. They demonstrate just how important promises are in our lives. These conversations focus primarily on the promises we make to one another. But the prayer that is part of this conversation really says more about God's promises to us. Everything, in fact, hinges on these promises. God promises to guide and direct our paths, to sustain us in our journey, and to dwell among and within us. To use classical Wesleyan language, God's promises are prevenient. They always precede our response. We make promises because God first made promises to us.

For the great reformer Martin Luther, the idea of promise provides the key to the gospel. He maintains that God only deals with human

2. *The United Methodist Book of Worship* (Nashville: The United Methodist Publishing House, 1992), 118.

beings through the "word of promise."[3] For John and Charles Wesley this means the "promise of love." This promise, like the delta at the mouth of a great river, fans out in all directions to nourish and enrich life. God promises love to us in the first place, and we love because God first loved us (1 John 4). Because we have received the promise of love we are able to love others (Matt 22:39). In this final conversation on the way of wisdom in the Wesleyan tradition, we explore God's promise of love and several of its life-shaping dimensions.[4]

First, *God promises to love us.* We talked about God's free and unbounded grace in our very first conversation with you. But more can always be said about the love that stands behind that grace. In their work entitled *Unbounded Love*, Clark Pinnock and Robert Brow reclaim the vision of a God of unbounded love.[5] Three broad themes provide the outline for their portrait of God. First, God's love extends to all. Second, the primary image of God in scripture is that of a loving parent, not a judge. Third, mutuality and openness characterize the posture of this biblical God. If this is our primary portrait of God, then the ramifications with regards to God's promise of love are rather monumental. God envelopes all people—indeed, all creation—in the wooing activity of this love. God surrounds and fills everyone and everything with love. This is the "playing field of life" from a Wesleyan perspective—time and space filled with love—and God promises to us that this will never end.

The God revealed in Jesus delights in goodness, beauty, and love, in all their various forms. God also takes pleasure in fulfilling the promises of love. The early Methodists sang about God's joy in such things:

---

3. Martin Luther, "*De captivitae babylonica* (1520)," in *Luther's Works, Volume 36, Word and Sacrament II,* ed. Abdel R. Wentz (Minneapolis: Augsburg Fortress Pub., 1959), 42.

4. This final chapter of the movement provides something of a segway into Movement 2 on wonder. Some of the dimensions of God's love described here find fuller expression in what follows, particularly in a discussion of the Wesleyan way of salvation.

5. Clark K. Pinnock and Robert C. Brow, *Unbounded Love: A Good News Theology for the 21st Century* (Eugene, OR: Wipf & Stock, 2000).

I bid you all my goodness prove,
My promises for all are free:
Come taste the manna of my love,
And let your soul delight in me.[6]

"Understood properly," Pinnock and Brow suggest, "God is practically irresistible. It is a mystery to us why anyone would reject [the God] who loves them so. Why would anyone reject the One whose very glory consists in everlasting love toward humans?"[7] Once the Wesleys experienced this kind of God, they made the pursuit of holiness—the fullest possible love of God and neighbor—their primary aim. J. Ernest Rattenbury observed that Charles Wesley's "subsequent spiritual life might be summed up compendiously in one phrase: 'a quest for love.'"[8] John shared this passion and wrote about it persistently.

The concluding stanzas of a hymn written by Charles soon after the brothers' poignant experience of God's love in 1738 capture a sense of the energy behind their common quest:

To love is all my wish,
I only live for this:
Grant me, Lord, my heart's desire,
There by faith forever dwell:
This I always will require
Thee and only thee to feel.

Thy power I pant to prove
Rooted and fixed in love,
Strengthened by thy Spirit's might,
Wise to fathom things divine,
What the length and breadth and height,
What the depth of love like thine.

Ah! Give me this to know
With all thy saints below.

6. Wesley, *Hymns and Sacred Poems* (1740), 2.
7. Pinnock and Brow, *Unbounded Love*, 12.
8. J. Ernest Rattenbury, *The Evangelical Doctrines of Charles Wesley's Hymns* (London: Epworth Press, 1954), 278.

Swells my soul to compass thee,
Gasps in thee to live and move,
Filled with all the deity,
All immersed and lost in love![9]

This hymn so powerfully expresses the reciprocal love that God's love inspires in each of us. God's promise of love includes the experiences of grace, forgiveness, union with Christ, aid, rest, peace, and perfect love. These are all words drawn from Charles Wesley's hymns about God's promises. We want to love in the same way we have been loved, and a whole host of God's collateral promises spill out from the quest for and experience of God's love in our lives.[10] These key themes—promises in and of themselves—reflect God's promise of love: God changes our hearts through love. God makes us like Christ through love. God produces radiant lives through love. Transformation, Christlikeness, and radiance characterize disciples of Jesus who seek to live the Wesleyan way. These are the promises of love.

Second, *God changes our hearts through love*. For both John and Charles Wesley, Psalm 51, particularly verses 10-12, strike an important keynote for their theology and practice:

Create in me a clean heart, O God,
and put a new and right spirit within me.
Do not cast me away from your presence,
and do not take your holy spirit from me.
Restore to me the joy of your salvation,
and sustain in me a willing spirit.

The Wesleys embedded these words deeply in their memories and imaginations and returned to them frequently. The God of this prayer creates, sustains, and restores—gifts central to the Wesleyan way. A clean heart and a right spirit define the reawakened child of God. The presence of this God in your life brings joy. John Wesley concludes

9. Wesley, *Hymns and Sacred Poems* (1739), 169.

10. See Paul W. Chilcote, *The Quest for Love Divine: Select Essays in Wesleyan Theology and Practice* (Eugene, OR: Cascade Books, 2022).

his sermon on "Christian Perfection" with a string of biblical citations (Deut 30:6, Psa 51:10, Ezek 36:25-26), all of which allude to God's promise to change our hearts. "Having therefore these promises, dearly beloved," he closes, "let us press toward the mark for the prize of the high calling of God in Christ Jesus."[11]

Given the fact that whatever is written on the heart reflects the true character of the person, God must restore, or transcribe, the heart fully. Many of Charles's hymns celebrate the heart of the believer—the heart upon which God has written the law of love. God writes on the heart, shapes the character, forms the disciple, restores the image of Christ in the child. In a hymn written for Elizabeth Carr, whom Charles baptized near Oxford in 1748, he prays:

> Father, all thy love reveal,
> Jesus all thy mind impart,
> Holy Ghost, renew, and dwell
> Forever in her heart.[12]

Most likely he drew his inspiration for the following hymn from a famous collect of the Anglican *Book of Common Prayer.* It joyfully anticipates God's transformation of the heart and the restoration of love.

> O for a heart to praise my God,
> A heart from sin set free!
> A heart that always feels thy blood,
> So freely spilt for me!
>
> A heart in every thought renewed
> And full of love divine,
> Perfect and right and pure and good,
> A copy, Lord, of thine.
>
> Thy nature, gracious Lord, impart;
> Come quickly from above;

11. Wesley, *Works*, 2:120–21.
12. Wesley, *Hymns and Sacred Poems* (1749), 2:246.

Write thy new name upon my heart,
Thy new, best name of Love.[13]

As S T Kimbrough has observed with regards to this hymn, "it is through the *steadfast love of God* that we are granted pure hearts. It is *God's love* that enables and sustains purity of heart. There is no way to purity and holiness without love!"[14] The Wesleys believed that no force in the universe is more powerful than love. Love is more powerful than hate. Love triumphs over evil. Love can conquer the disobedient heart. Love never coerces. Love never fails. They prayed consistently for God's love to fill their own hearts, and not theirs only, but the hearts of every child of God.

Third, *God makes us like Christ through love*. Transformed followers of Jesus will be like him. Those who bear the image of Christ conform not only to him in heart, but in mind and life as well. To grow into the person God has called you to be—to be fully human—means to be Christlike. In a journal entry dated November 4, 1737 (note that this is prior to Aldersgate), John Wesley records that he "heard an excellent sermon at St. Antholin's on holiness, or likeness to God."[15] He celebrates the preacher's exposition of Matthew 10:25, in particular, "it is enough for the disciple to be like the teacher." Throughout the entirety of his life, John believed that those who follow Jesus ought to think, speak, and act like him. Charles, as one might expect, put this central concept of conformity to Christ in lyrical form. He explicitly connects the transformation or restoration of the heart with Christlikeness:

We rest on His word
We shall here be restored
To His image; the servant shall be as his Lord.[16]

13. Wesley, *Hymns and Sacred Poems* (1742), 30–31.

14. S T Kimbrough, Jr., *A Heart to Praise My God* (Nashville: Abingdon Press, 2000), 140.

15. S T Kimbrough, Jr. and Kenneth G. C. Newport, *The Manuscript Journal of the Reverend Charles Wesley, M.A.*, 2 vols. (Nashville: Kingswood Books, 2007), 1:93.

16. Wesley, *Hymns and Sacred Poems* (1749), 2:179.

This call to conformity to Christ defines the disciple—it characterizes the Christian who is altogether God's—and it also reflects God's promise. In virtually every hymn in which this phrase of Charles appears—"the servant shall be as his Lord"—it implies both a demand and a gift. "I stay me on thy faithful word," cries the follower of Christ leaning on God's promise. "The servant shall be as his Lord."[17] In the hymn "Prisoners of Hope" this statement of vocation and promise functions as the refrain for the concluding stanzas:

Thou wilt perform thy faithful word:
"The servant shall be as his Lord."

We only hang upon thy word,
"The servant shall be as his Lord."[18]

But what does it mean to be like Jesus according to the Wesleys? How do they define Christlikeness? First, the heart of those who are Christlike rests in God. The Wesleys drew this image, similar to abiding, from great Lutheran Pietists like Gerhard Tersteegen. John translated one of his brilliant texts into English:

Thou hidden love of God, whose height,
Whose depth unfathomed, no man knows;
I see from far thy beauteous light,
Inly I sigh for thy repose;
My heart is pained, nor can it be
At rest, till it finds rest in thee.[19]

The Christlike follower of Jesus abides in God's love; God's promise of love provides soulful rest.

Christlikeness implies having the mind of Christ. In his sermon on "The Mystery of Iniquity," John Wesley provides one of his most terse

17. Wesley, *Hymns and Sacred Poems* (1742), 80.

18. Wesley, *Hymns and Sacred Poems* (1742), 234.

19. Wesley, *Hymns and Sacred Poems* (1739), 78–80. Hear the echoes here of St. Augustine's well-known image of "restlessness" drawn from the opening paragraph of *The Confessions*.

definitions. Real Christians, he claims, are who "have the mind which was in Christ, and walk as he walked."[20] In the closing paragraph of "The Unity of the Divine Being," he proclaims:

> See that ye love God; next your neighbour, every child of man. From this fountain let every tempter, every affection, every passion flow. So shall that "mind be in you which was also in Christ Jesus". Let all your thoughts, words, and actions spring from this. So shall you "inherit the kingdom prepared for you from the beginning of the world."[21]

Charles expands this definition of Christlikeness in a hymn that conjoins the "mind" of Philippians 2 with the "action" of James 1:

> Thy mind throughout my life be shown,
> While listening to the wretch's cry,
> The widow's and the orphan's groan,
> On mercy's wings I swiftly fly
> The poor and helpless to relieve,
> My life, my all for them to give.[22]

Those who are Christlike demonstrate the mind of Christ by putting their love into action.

Christlikeness can be seen in "singleness of eye"—the pure and simple intention for love to reign in your life. In 1789, near the end of his life's journey, John Wesley wrote a sermonic essay based on Matthew 6:22-23 entitled "On a Single Eye."[23] In this exposition of the Christlike life he makes three basic points. (1) Holiness or Christlike living entails purity of intention. (2) He complains that nominal Christians—those he elsewhere describes as "almost Christians"—compromise the witness of the church. (3) Riches distract disciples of Jesus from true Christlikeness and simplicity of life.

---

20. Wesley, *Works*, 2:467.
21. Wesley, *Works*, 4:71.
22. Charles Wesley, *Short Hymns on Select Passages of the Holy Scriptures*, 2 vols. (Bristol: Farley, 1762), 2:380.
23. Wesley, *Works*, 4:120–30.

He attributes these ideas and concerns to those great and formative influences in his life—Thomas à Kempis, Jeremy Taylor, and William Law. He expresses his deep desire for all the children of God to strive for simplicity and singleness of eye. He admonishes his followers to love as they have been loved in Christ. He makes love, essentially, the key to life in all its wonder. "How great a thing it is to be a Christian," he writes, "to be a real, inward, scriptural Christian! Conformed in heart and life to the will of God! Who is sufficient for these things? . . . '[L]et your eye be single', that your 'whole body may be full of light'!"[24]

Finally, *God produces radiant lives through love.* Christlike followers of Jesus shine to God's glory. You must sing about radiance. Simple prose just does not do God's light justice. So Charles Wesley sings:

Clothed with Christ aspire to shine,
    Radiance he of light divine;
Beam of the eternal beam,
    He in God, and God in him!
Strive we him in us to see,
    Transcript of the deity.[25]

For the Wesleys, Christ is the true and only light of the world whose radiance transcends all darkness. When this light floods the soul, all manner of darkness vanishes. They pray that all people might experience the in-breaking of the glorious light of the One "whose glory fills the skies," "shining to the perfect day."[26]

God's promise of love finds ultimate expression in an overwhelming sense of God's presence. Holiness equals love; love equals holiness, and all is miracle as the faithful live out their lives on the foundation of God's grace. The Wesleyan way of wisdom moves seamlessly into the Wesleyan way of wonder. You get a clear sense of this segway in words of admonition that Mary Fletcher shared with her fellow sojourners and disciples in Christ:

24. Wesley, *Works*, 4:130.
25. Wesley, *Hymns and Sacred Poems* (1739), 178.
26. Wesley, *Hymns and Sacred Poems* (1740), 25.

Be earnest with the Lord, that his love may fill your heart, as the Scripture expresses it, the love of God, shed abroad in your hearts by the Holy Ghost, given unto you. If you get your hearts full of the love of God, you will find that is the oil by which the lamp of faith will be ever kept burning. . . . Pray, my friends, pray much for this love; and remember that word, "He that dwelleth in love dwelleth in God, and God in him!"[27]

27. Quoted in Mary Tooth, *A Letter to the Loving and Beloved People of the Parish of Madeley [by Mary Fletcher]* (Shiffnal: Printed by A. Edmonds, n.d.), 17–18.

Reflection Questions

Conversation 4 (Love)

1. What part of this Conversation spoke most to you? Why is it important for you to hear this right now?

2. How has the experience of God's love changed your life? Where has God "shown up" for you?

3. How is God working in your life right now to shape you into a more loving person?

MOVEMENT 2

The Way of Wonder

– Introduction –

When we move upward in Wesleyan formation, we live in wonder. Wonder is a consequence of wisdom. Charles Wesley sang about how we are "lost in wonder, love and praise" when we experience the love of God in its fullness—the love that exceeds all other loves.[1] This, he said, is our experience when we cast our crowns (our full consecration) before God in the culmination of the new creation. Grace triumphs in the end as all things are made new in love—the ultimacy of redemption (Eph 1:9-10). The life of God in the human soul is wonder-full.

The root meaning of salvation is wholeness, what Jesus described as abundant life (John 10:10). When the Wesleys arranged their theology as a way of salvation, it was their way of connecting faith to our life journey. From the outset theirs was a lived theology, with a soteriological core rooted in Christ that generates its substance and spirit—redemption and joy, holiness and happiness. This wholeness is built into the essence of life, into creation itself. Parker Palmer calls it a hidden wholeness, both to underscore the mystery of salvation, but also to reveal that we must be engaged in finding and enacting the spiritual life God intends for us. The Wesleys understood the mystery of life similarly and celebrated it in their theology.[2] Doing so is an experience of wonder.

The theme of wonder pervades Christian theology, the great theologians of the church taking their lead from the Bible, of course,

1. Wesley, *Redemption Hymns*, 12.

2. Parker Palmer, *A Hidden Wholeness* (San Francisco: Josey Bass, 2004).

and the *mysterium tremendum* (awe-inspiring mystery) of God revealed there. The grand narrative that reaches from creation through redemption to the fullest possible restoration demonstrates how human beings are drawn irresistibly to the glory, beauty, and majesty as well as the blessing and redeeming nature of God. From the Torah to the Gospels, awe and wonder abound.

"Who is like you, O Lord, among the gods? Who is like you, majestic in holiness, awesome in splendor, doing wonders" (Exod 15:11). "Amazement seized all of them," Luke records, "and they glorified God and were filled with fear, saying, 'We have seen incredible things today'" (5:26). A delightful example of understatement. But the psalmist specializes in wonder. "The whole earth is filled with awe at your wonders; where morning dawns, where evening fades, you call forth songs of joy" (65:8 NIV).

We perceive renewed interest in a sense of wonder in our day. Within the Christian family this owes much to the contemplative tradition and the discoveries of science. We are learning anew how to contemplate the wonder of God, God's creation, and the adventurous journey of our own lives. The Catholic mystical tradition informed these kinds of discoveries for the Wesleys. But John, in particular, also exhibited a keen interest in the rise of science in his own time. He wrote about its amazing discoveries and even incorporated some of them into early Methodist practices. Not only do we find wonder as we contemplate the biblical witness, we also experience it in creation through the lenses of the James Webb telescope. How can we not stand in awe and wonder as we ponder the images drawn from more than 100 billion galaxies, each of which contains 100 billion stars.

Wesleyans plumb the depths of wonder, therefore, in both creation and redemption, the twin expressions of God's grace. Creation evokes wonder in an obvious way; the wonder of redemption, perhaps, requires more explanation. Salvation at its root means wholeness, what Jesus described as abundant life (John 10:10). Albert Outler described the doctrine of salvation as the Wesleys' "axial theme."[3] Everything in

3. See Albert C. Outler, *Theology in the Wesleyan Spirit* (Nashville: Tidings Press, 1975).

their theology revolves around salvation. It is no surprise that when the Wesleys preached and sang about redemption or new creation, they described it as "the way of salvation."[4] In other words, they connected faith to our life journey. From the outset, theirs was a lived theology, with a soteriological core rooted in Christ that generates its substance and spirit—redemption and joy; holiness and happiness. This wholeness is built into the essence of life, into creation itself. John and Charles Wesley understood all these connections and celebrated them in their lived theology.

It is important to note that the Wesleys believed their scriptural way of salvation generated living faith, not simply affirmed faith. Intellectual ascent does not evoke wonder for most people. But love that brings you to life wraps everyone in wonder. Living into salvation also carries the redeemed into greater degrees of wonder. The Annual Conference of 1746 captured this dynamism in the phrase "salvation begun, salvation continued, and salvation finished."[5] Little wonder that John Wesley described this journey as "the way to heaven."[6] We believe that we need to recover wonder in theology via a way of salvation as never before. In contrast to other forms of Methodist theology today that lay claim on the Wesleyan tradition, we believe that theology true to the Wesleys begins, continues, and ends in wonder.

So what does wonder look like for those who seek to understand and live their faith through a Wesleyan lens? Four conversations around creation, redemption, sustenance, and restoration provide entry points into the way of wonder.

---

4. See Wesley, *Works*, 2:153–69.

5. John Wesley, *The Works of John Wesley, Volume 10, The Methodist Societies,* ed. Henry D. Rack (Nashville: Abingdon Press, 2011), 175.

6. He used the phrase in the Preface to his Sermons on Several Occasions. See John Wesley, *The Works of John Wesley, Volume 1, Sermons I, 1-33*, ed. Albert C. Outler (Nashville: Abingdon Press, 1984), 38–45; cf. Steve Harper, *The Way to Heaven: The Gospel According to John Wesley* (Grand Rapids: Zondervan, 2003).

- First, the Wesleyan way of salvation begins with creation, not sin. The Wesleys affirmed that God creates human beings in God's image and embraces us all as beloved children. Our conversation begins in the grandeur of creation.

- Second, regardless, we all know that something is not right. Despite the image of God stamped on our very being, brokenness and alienation characterize our life with God and others. God's provision for us in this mess reveals the liberation of redemption.

- Third, God not only brings reconciliation to God's beloved children, God sustains us on our journey of life. We will explore together how the delight of sustenance elicits gratitude and how the Wesleyan means of grace fill our hearts with love.

- Fourth, Wesleyan theology is a "full circle theology." It begins with creation and circles back to new creation as God works in our lives to restore God's original intention and design. Love is the keynote in the glory of restoration.

Charles Wesley opens the hymn he wrote on the day of his conversion (Pentecost, May 21, 1738) with a profound question: "Where shall my wondering soul begin?"[7] Creation, redemption, sustenance, and restoration are not bad starting points. Let's begin there together.

7. Wesley, *Hymns and Sacred Poems* (1739), 101.

Conversation 5

The Grandeur of Creation

It was a short conversation, but mind-blowing. David Wilkinson, a dear friend, has double doctor's degrees, one in theoretical astrophysics and the other in systematic theology. Paul had read his book *God, Time, & Stephen Hawking* about a decade after its original release and had a lot of questions.

"In your book you say there are 100 billion galaxies we can now see and each has about 100 billion stars!"

"Yep. That's right," he said.

"The only thing is," he continued. "My book is now outdated. Most of my colleagues now believe we can see well over 200 billion galaxies."

Wonder begins in creation. It commences as we observe all that God has made. As David put it, "Heaven is declaring God's glory; the sky is proclaiming his handiwork" (Psa 19:1). The Wesleys agreed. In his *Explanatory Notes Upon the Old Testament*, John commented on David's words, writing that "the book of the creatures shows us the power and Godhead of the Creator."[8] Charles expressed the same sentiment, "Be thou by all thy works adored!"[9] Praise begins in the wonder of creation.

Wesleyan theology begins as natural theology. Like the monastic tradition of St. Francis of Assisi, it recognizes creation as the "first

8. John Wesley, *Explanatory Notes upon the Old Testament* (Bristol: William Pine, 1765), Introduction to Genesis.

9. Wesley, *Hymns and Sacred Poems*, 189.

bible." It is not too much to say that creation gives rise to the "second bible" that we call Holy Scripture. The Wesleys view the Bible as the revelation of a larger reality—the story of God's Story—a revelation that includes the visible and invisible dimensions of life (see Col 1:16).

In developing his natural theology, John Wesley drew from the well of the wisdom tradition. In 1763 he published a compellation of scientific knowledge about the world as it was known and understood at that time. The title itself demonstrates his interest in the interface of religion and science and its connection with wisdom: *A survey of the wisdom of God in the creation: or a compendium of natural philosophy.*[10] He develops his theology, in other words, in dialogue with his study of the natural world. The discoveries of science enlarged his understanding of the world and enriched his beliefs and practices. This integrative approach also saved him from obscurantism and the perpetuation of ideas and ways of understanding life that were no longer credible. It guarded him and his followers from "doing harm." The sciences only enhance the wonder of all that surrounds us in life. In this conversation, we explore the various aspects of Wesleyan theology that underscore the grandeur of creation.

First, *in Wesleyan natural theology everything begins with God.* Before we exit the first creation story (Gen 1:1–2:4), we come face to face with the Holy Trinity. God is intimately and intricately involved. Wesley saw this in the writer's use of the word *Elohim* to describe God.[11] The Father is the parent from whose heart creation comes. The Son is the universal Christ who made all things (John 1:3, 1:9). The Spirit hovered over creation like a mother hen, cooling and caring for it (Gen 1:2). From the moment God said, "Let there be light," the cosmos evolved in holiness through its likeness with God.

For too long, the Trinity has been seen as so inexplicable as to be

10. John Wesley, *A survey of the wisdom of God in the creation: or a compendium of natural philosophy,* 2 vols. (Bristol: William Pine, 1763).

11. Wesley, *Old Testament Notes,* comment in Introduction to Genesis.

irrelevant.[12] The Wesleys did not believe or teach this.[13] Rather, they saw the Trinity as the active energy running through time and space, "one God in three persons," in a divine dance (*perichoresis*) that makes and saves the world. The nature of God (love) defines the nature of creation (lovely and loveable). These ideas come to full expression in Charles Wesley's "Hymn on the Trinity," a hymn that must be read or sung in its entirety:

Father, in whom we live,
In whom we are and move,
The glory, power, and praise receive
Of thy creating love.
Let all the angel-throng
Give thanks to God on high,
While earth repeats the joyful song,
And echoes to the sky.

Incarnate deity,
Let all the ransomed race
Render in thanks their lives to thee
For thy redeeming grace;
The grace to sinners showed,
Ye heavenly choirs proclaim,
And cry Salvation to our God,
Salvation to the Lamb.

Spirit of holiness,
Let all thy saints adore
Thy sacred energy, and bless
Thine heart-renewing power

12. Fortunately, this is changing, and scholars and practitioners of the faith are exploring the Trinity with fresh energy. See Richard Rohr, *The Divine Dance: The Trinity and Your Transformation* (New Kensington, PA: Whitaker House, 2016) for a helpful exploration of this recovery.

13. See Paul W. Chilcote, "'Practical Christology' in John and Charles Wesley," in *Methodist Christology: From the Wesleys to the Twenty-First Century*, ed. Jason Vickers (Nashville: Wesley Foundery Books, 2020), 3–35.

Not angel-tongues can tell
Thy love's ecstatic height,
The glorious joy unspeakable,
The beatific sight.

Eternal Triune Lord,
Let all the hosts above,
Let all the sons of men record,
And dwell upon thy love;
When heaven and earth are fled
Before thy glorious face,
Sing all the saints thy love hath made,
Thine everlasting praise.[14]

As can be seen from this hymn, the Wesleys root their theology in the Trinity in a soteriological sense.[15] They view all three persons as fully coinherent, equal, and participatory in the way of salvation.[16] We will look at Jesus Christ (redemption) and the Spirit (sustenance) in the immediately subsequent conversations, but we focus on God as Parent for a moment in this exploration of the grandeur of creation.

Historically, masculine terms like "Father" have been used more generally to describe the first person of the Trinity. The Bible, however, often reveals the divine feminine. John Wesley noted this in his comment on Genesis 1:2: "As the hen gathereth her chicken under her wings, and hovers over them, to warm and cherish them, Matt. xxiii, 37 as the eagle stirs up her nest, and fluttereth over her young, ('tis the same word that is here used) Deut. xxxii, 11."[17] God is "Mother" as well as Father. This makes "Parent" a good way to view God, particularly in relation to creation. For one thing, *parent* expresses capacity for likeness.

---

14. Wesley, *Redemption Hymns*, 44–45.

15. Geoffrey Wainwright, "Trinitarian Theology and Wesleyan Holiness," in *Orthodox and Wesleyan Spirituality*, ed. S T Kimbrough, Jr. (Yonkers, NY: St. Vladimir's Seminary Press, 2002), 59–80.

16. Randy L. Maddox, *Responsible Grace: John Wesley's Practical Theology* (Nashville: Kingswood Books, 1994), 139.

17. John Wesley, *Explanatory Notes upon the New Testament* (Bristol: William Pine, 1765), comment on Gen 1:2.

God creates all things in the likeness of God. As a parent, God reveals the relational nature (I-Thou) of reality. As a parent God expresses the intent to walk with the creation through thick and thin, sustaining it and rescuing it. In the Trinity hymn cited above, according to Charles, the response of God's child is quite simply to "dwell upon thy love"—the love of a faithful and trustworthy parent.

Clearly, the Trinity is where Wesleyan theology begins, both in relation to the nature of God but also in relation to our response to God. We love because God first loved us, in both creation and redemption (1 John 4:19), and to be a faithful child means to share that love freely with others. In this regard, creation serves as a lens through which we see our beloved Parent, God in three persons, blessed Trinity.

Second, *creation reveals universality*. God created (and is creating) the heavens and the earth. That's everyone and everything, from the smallest particle to the farthest star. God is present in genes and galaxies. St. Francis celebrated God's presence and activity in creation by purportedly saying that God is doing cartwheels in creation. This visual metaphor is increasingly affirmed by the sciences.[18] This idea of God's presence and ongoing activity in creation is usually known as "universality."[19] This is precisely what St. Paul had in mind when he quoted the ancient Greek poet Aratus in Acts 17:28, "In God, we live, move, and exist. As some of your own poets said, 'We are his offspring.'"

The very first verse of the Bible—God created "the heavens and the earth" (Gen 1:1)—inspired John Wesley to develop his theology around the axis of creation. In his sermon, "On the Omnipresence of God," he observes that "heaven and earth includes the whole universe, the whole extent of space, created or uncreated, and all that is therein."[20] This provides the theological basis for Peter's claim that God

18. Ilia Delio, *The Hours of the Universe: Reflections on God, Science, and the Human Journey* (Maryknoll, NY: Orbis Books, 2021). Delio founded the Center for Christogenesis to study the theology/science interface further.

19. We will look at universality from a different perspective in the next conversation.

20. Wesley, *Works*, 4:44.

is "not wanting anyone to perish" (2 Pet 3:9). Paul extends this affirmation to the whole creation (Rom 8:21). The universality of a God-created universe is the motivation for a God-redeemed cosmos. What God wills, God accomplishes.

Third, *creation manifests oneness*. The Wesleys recognized the unity of all things, both with respect to their common Maker, but also with respect to their interconnectedness.[21] Because everyone and everything partakes of the divine nature, there is a created accountability among all beings—an existence in which every part of creation contributes to the wellbeing of every other part. Today we call this ecotheology.[22] Here again, Wesleyan theology demonstrates its kinship with the wisdom tradition in general, and Celtic and indigenous theological traditions in particular.[23] Without any question whatsoever, the Wesleys would be engaged in the current efforts to save the earth—efforts that emerge from a sacred sense of oneness. We see this in the following ways.

We see oneness in God's charge for humans to have dominion over the earth (Gen 1:27). Great harm has been done up to the present by a gross misinterpretation of dominion as domination. The truth of the idea has to do with stewardship and tending the earth in ways that lead to flourishing and thriving. John Wesley understood dominion in this way, as God's call for humans to "replenish the earth, in which God has set man to be the servant of his providence."[24] Dominion generates; it does not destroy. It arises from our recognition that we are God's servants and co-laborers in the ongoing life of the cosmos.

We see oneness further in Jesus' exhortation for us to love our neighbors as we love ourselves (Matt 22:39). This is the only verse

---

21. Mark K. Olson, "From the Beginning to the End: John Wesley's Doctrine of Creation," wesleyscholar.com, March 1, 2031; https://wesleyscholar.com/from-the-beginning-to-the-end-john-wesleys-doctrine-of-creation/; accessed January 16, 2023.

22. Kiara A. Jorgenson and Alan G. Padgett, eds., *Ecotheology: A Christian Conversation* (Grand Rapids: Wm. B. Eerdmans, 2020).

23. John Philip Newell, *The Rebirthing of God: Christianity's Struggle for New Beginnings* (Woodstock, VT: Skylight Paths, 2015), chapter one, "Reconnecting with the Earth."

24. Wesley, *Old Testament Notes*, comment on Gen 1:27.

he took from the holiness code of his Jewish heritage (Lev 19:18). From the example of his own life, we know that our neighbors are not only other humans, but also all that God has made.[25] Oneness means entering deeply into life, a compassionate interaction with others that St. Paul describes as having mutual concern for each other. "If one part suffers, all the parts suffer with it; if one part gets the glory, all parts celebrate with it" (1 Cor 12:26). This care for one another, as John Wesley noted, is given to all but especially to those who are too often deprived of it.[26]

Fourth, *God creates all things good*. This thread runs through the first creation story as the writer uses the word seven times, and from there through the rest of the Bible. The idea emerges from the likeness of the creation to the Creator. God is good; all that God made is too. The idea of goodness reflects the moral excellency of the cosmos. This seminal reality led Pierre Teilhard de Chardin to conceive the essence of the universe as love. Likewise, it moved Thomas Berry to recognize its holiness.[27] John Wesley carried the same idea forward, noting that the creation "'Twas exactly as he designed it, and it was fit to answer the end for which he designed it."[28]

When we come to the goodness of creation, we arrive at a Wesleyan hallmark: original righteousness. Some Christian theology begins, at least in tone, with original sin. But the Bible does not begin there; neither did the Wesleys. They began with original blessing (Gen 2:3), a consequence of God's recognition that the whole of creation was "supremely good" (Gen 1:31). Choosing to begin with original righteousness, the Wesleys consciously choose a theological starting

25. Walter Brueggemann, *God, Neighbor, Empire: The Excess of Divine Fidelity and the Command of Common Good* (Waco, TX: Baylor University Press, 2016) studies the idea of neighborliness in detail, extending it beyond human beings.

26. Wesley, *New Testament Notes*, comment on 1 Cor 12:24.

27. Pierre Teilhard de Chardin, *The Divine Milieu* (originally published in French in 1927, this is available in multiple English translations) and Thomas Berry, *The Sacred Universe: Earth, Spirituality, and Religion in the Twenty-first Century* (New York: Columbia University Press, 2009).

28. Wesley, *Old Testament Notes*, comment on Gen 1:3.

point older than that of original sin. But more, they contextualized their theological system within original goodness to show not only the origin of creation but also its *telos*.[29] Their understanding of the life developed in relation to this perspective.

We live at a time in which many are recovering a theology of original righteousness.[30] We hope this book will contribute to the recovery by including the Wesleys and the Wesleyan tradition among the sources for understanding our fundamental goodness, a goodness which saturates the cosmos and makes it beautiful.[31] Indeed, it is a light that darkness cannot extinguish (John 1:5). As we will see in the next conversation, it is original righteousness that provides the basis for redemption. For now, we highlight it as a theological factor and force that fuels the fire of love.

Fifth, *creation is progressively ordered*. The story of creation in scripture describes its evolution using the metaphor of "days"—the unfolding epochs of creation over billions of years. God's creative action continues, of course, with ongoing expansion into our day and beyond. In the Celtic tradition, which we believe exerted some influence over the Wesleys, creation is not only an event, it functions as a paradigm as well. In this larger sense, the days of creation serve as metaphors for the stages of life, individually and collectively.[32] Humanity plays its part and finds its place in this larger, unfolding story of creation.

We see this creation paradigm in human development as we move from birth, to childhood, to adolescence, to early adulthood, to our middle years, and on to old age and death. We see it similarly in faith development as we move from innocence, to awakening, to passion,

---

29. Colin W. Williams, *John Wesley's Theology Today* (Nashville: Abingdon Press, 1960), 56.

30. See Matthew Fox, *Original Blessing: A Primer in Creation Spirituality*, rev. ed. (New York: J. P. Tarcher/Penguin, 2000), 18–35 where Fox demonstrates how original blessing antedates and is a more widely held view than original sin.

31. David Rainey, "Beauty in Creation: John Wesley's Natural Philosophy," *Wesley and Methodist Studies* 9, 1 (2017): 18–35.

32. J. Philip Newell, *One Foot in Eden: A Celtic View of the Stages of Life* (Mahweh, NJ: Paulist Press, 1999).

to commitment, to wisdom, and finally into holy dying. John Wesley experienced both dimensions of growth and viewed theology in this life-oriented way. The natural order of maturation and the spiritual way of salvation cannot be separated because they both arise from and exist in God. Growth in grace is natural because we are within an evolving cosmos. E. Stanley Jones saw and proclaimed this unity, pointing out that "the Way" is inscribed in our cells, nerves, tissues, and fibers.[33] In every way (spirit, soul, and body) we are made by God and for God. Creation, the first Bible, tells us so!

To use an image drawn from C. S. Lewis's Narnia Chronicles, through Aslan God sang everything into existence. This actually reflects a more accurate translation of the Genesis account of creation. It should be no surprise to learn that Charles Wesley understood God's creative work in the universe through the metaphor of harmony. That is just an expansion of the image of sound and song. We come to know who we are most fully when we find our place in the greater harmony of God that surrounds us in life. Charles encourages us to find our voice in God's great song of life.

Thou God of harmony and love,
Whose name transports the saints above,
        And lulls the ravished spheres,
On thee in feeble strains I call,
And mix my humble voice with all
        The heavenly choristers.

If well I know the tuneful art
To captivate a human heart,
        The glory, Lord, be thine:
A servant of thy blessed will
I here devote my utmost skill,
        To sound the praise divine.

Suffice for this the season past:
I come, great God, to learn at last

33. E. Stanley Jones, *The Way* (Nashville: Abingdon Press, 1946). Weeks 1-6 unpack his natural theology, largely that of the Wesleys.

The lesson of thy grace,
Teach me the new, the gospel song,
And let my hand, my heart, my tongue
Move only to thy praise.[34]

This song culminates in a new creation. It includes restoration of the first creation (described metaphorically as a new heaven and a new earth), but with dimensions not seen in the original (see Rev 22:5). Caught up, as they were, in the glory of God in the current creation, it is no surprise that the Wesleys wanted everyone to live abundantly enroute to the new. This desire produced the redemptive design of their theology, which we will explore in the next three conversations.

34. Wesley, *Redemption Hymns*, 34–35.

Reflection Questions

Conversation 5 (Creation)

1. What part of this Conversation spoke most to you? Why is it important for you to hear this right now?

2. How have you found the creation to be formational in helping you live the Christian life?

3. Where does creation-care fit into your faith? What groups are you involved with directly or as a donor?

Conversation 6

The Dignity of Redemption

Steve and Jeannie had an experience while at Duke University that sets the stage for this conversation on redemption. She bought him an expensive pen to take notes in his coursework and research. No matter where he was writing, it would be a sign of her love and support during his doctoral studies.

One evening he reached for the pen, to take notes while reading, but it was not there. He looked in obvious places, but still no pen. That commenced a search all over the place, a quest that suspended his study plans in an effort to find the lost pen. But the pen was nowhere to be found! There was nothing else for Steve to do but tell Jeannie when she returned from a Bible study meeting, "I lost the pen you gave me."

Upon doing so, Jeannie reached into her purse and said, "You mean this one? I picked it up on my way out the door to be sure I had something to write with at the meeting." Steve could not believe his eyes. The lost pen was found. It was home!

This experience illustrates much of what we want to say about redemption in this conversation. That experience defines redemption for us. We go in search, a relentless search for things that are valuable to us. What has become lost must be found. We do not search for junk; we redeem pearls of great price. God searches for us for the same reason. We are God's beloved. Even one lost sheep is unacceptable. God has moved heaven and earth to redeem us.

Redemption defines the Wesleyan way. It happens because the thing being rescued has prior value. The last conversation about Wesleyan natural theology established the inestimable value of creation, of everyone and everything. But as St. Paul notes, creation is groaning for its redemption (Rom 8:22). When viewed in relation to the grand creation of which it is a part, redemption is exactly what we would expect it to be. Quite simply, it is the will and work of God. According to Jesus, God actually wills a great treasure for us all: life in God's loving reign (Matt 13:44). This treasure is there, but we must unearth it. It must not remain hidden.

Once discovered, this great prize overwhelms us by the wonder of the freedom it reveals. "If the Son makes you free," St. John tells us, "you will be free indeed" (John 8:36). When Charles Wesley put this discovery into poetry, he had to use a galloping meter. The excitement was just too much to contain:

> The blessing is free:
> So, Lord, let it be;
> I yield that thy love should be given to me.
> I freely receive
> What thou freely dost give,
> And consent in thy love, in thy Eden, to live.[1]

In this conversation we celebrate the wonder of redemption, the freedom it entails, its liberating effect on our lives, and the response it elicits.

First, *redemption is liberation (recovery, restoration)*. The redemptive focus of Wesleyan theology makes it, by definition, liberation theology. Wesley's hymn originally entitled "Free Grace" is one of the most significant lyrical expositions of redemptive liberation in the history of Christian song. It treats this theme in a magisterial way and identifies liberation as one of the most important experiences related to redemption in Christ.

1. Wesley, *Redemption Hymns*, 7.

Long my imprisoned spirit lay,
Fast bound in sin and nature's night:
Thine eye diffused a quick'ning ray;
I woke; the dungeon flamed with light;
My chains fell off, my heart was free,
I rose, went forth, and followed thee.[2]

In his letter to the Galatians, St. Paul put this very simply: "Christ has set us free for freedom" (5:1). To this biblical message, John Wesley added the exhortation, "Stand fast therefore in the liberty."[3]

Second, *there are two overarching realities associated with this liberation.* Two critical aspects of Wesleyan theology hold the various elements of redemption together. The first reality is *the redeeming love of God*. Thomas Jay Oord rightly notes that "few theologians consider love their orienting concern."[4] The Wesleys did. They did so because they believed theology emerges from our fundamental understanding of God's nature. For them, God's nature is love. John Wesley described love as God's "reigning attribute that sheds an amiable glory on all his other perfections."[5]

But the Wesleys' concept of love, as we have seen, is not abstract. Love acts. Love acts redemptively. Just as creation reveals the restorative (unifying) energy of the cosmos, the Bible reveals God's re-gathering intent. God's redeeming love draws all things together. "When I am lifted up from the earth," claims Jesus, "I will draw everyone to me" (John 12:32). St. Paul echoes this vision in his letter to the Ephesians. "This is what God planned for the climax of all times: to bring all things together in Christ, the things in heaven along with the things on earth" (1:10 CEB). Commenting on this verse, John Wesley notes:

> —in this last administration of God's fullest grace, which took place when the time appointed was fully come. He might gather together

2. Wesley, *Hymns and Sacred Poems* (1739), 118.

3. Wesley, *New Testament Notes*, comment on Gal 5:1.

4. Thomas Jay Oord, *Pluriform Love: An Open and Relational Theology of Well-being* (Grasmere, ID: SacraSage Press, 2022), 205.

5. Wesley, *New Testament Notes*, comment on 1 John 4:8.

> in Christ—Might re-capitulate, re-unite, and place in order again under Christ, their common Head. All things which are in heaven and on earth—All angels and men, whether living or dead, in the Lord.[6]

In her book *The Theology of Love*, Mildred Bangs Wynkoop wrote that "the ultimate meaning of redemption is the restoration of fellowship with God."[7] In Wesleyan theology love is active in bringing God's plan to pass.

This begs the question, "How does this happen?" The answer to this question brings us to the second overarching reality: *the redeeming grace of God.* Grace is love enacted. Grace is the means by which God manifests saving love. Charles Wesley described it as "amazing love, that thou, my God, shouldst die for me"—indeed, for all.[8] Within the context of the way of salvation, grace unfolds as preventing, converting, sanctifying, and glorifying in its operations. To be clear, these are not four kinds of grace. Grace is grace is grace. Essentially, grace is God's offer of relationship. But love enacts relationally in our lives in multiple ways depending on where we stand in our relationship with God. We experience God's love as grace in different ways at different times. St. John describes this as "grace upon grace" (John 1:16), a phrase that pictures one ocean with wave after wave coming onshore.

In Conversation 1 we looked together at grace from the divine side with regard to the upward call of Christ. In this Conversation we view grace in terms of its effects as we respond to this manifestation of God's love in our lives. That is, we focus on the human side of a theology of grace. God, of course, remains primary. But exploring the operation of grace in our lives does not diminish its source. We experience the wonder of redemption through our evolving relationship with Christ. Our loving and dynamic relationship with God unfolds in an organic

---

6. Wesley, *New Testament Notes*, comment on Eph 1:10.

7. Mildred Bangs Wynkoop, *A Theology of Love: The Dynamic of Wesleyanism,* 2nd ed. (Kansas City: Beacon Hill, 2015), loc 5735. Wynkoop's work helped many recognize the centrality of love in Wesleyan theology.

8. Wesley, *Hymns and Sacred Poems* (1739), 117.

way as we respond to God's grace in our lives. Many of John's sermons and Charles's hymns explore the wonder of grace in our lives.[9]

We begin with *preventing or prevenient grace*. The Wesleys believed that God reaches out to us in love before we have any awareness of God's presence or action. Grace envelopes, or surrounds, every person. Grace comes before anything else. First and foremost, God reaches out to us in love. The Wesleys, therefore, describe this as prevenient grace—grace "which comes before" (the actual meaning of the term—*pre* before and *ventus* to come). God surrounds us with love before we have any awareness of it and prior to our acceptance of it. Here is how Wesley describes preventing grace in his sermon:

> If we take this in its utmost extent it will include all that is wrought in the soul by what is frequently termed "natural conscience," but more properly "preventing grace." This includes all the "drawings" of "the Father," the desires after God, which, if we yield to them increase more and more; all that "light" wherewith the Son of God "enlighteneth everyone that cometh into the world," showing every person "to do justly, to love mercy, and to walk humbly with his God;" all the convictions which God's Spirit from time to time works in every child of earth.[10]

Light figures prominently as the primary image for this grace in the hymns of Charles Wesley.

> Lightened by thy interior ray
> Thee every child of Adam may
> His unknown God adore,
> And following close thy secret grace
> Emerge into that glorious place
> Where darkness is no more.[11]

---

9. See Steve Harper, "Wesley's Sermons as Spiritual Formation Documents," *Methodist History* 26 (April 1988): 131–38.

10. Wesley, *Works*, 2:156–57.

11. Wesley, *Scripture Hymns*, 2:238.

Prevenient grace, according to the Wesleys, restores a measure of free will or the *imago Dei* (Gen 1:26-28) lost in the fall, making possible our recognition of grace and our response to it as an act of freedom, not imposition. This is the source of our responsibility, therefore, in the process of salvation. We partner with God as we move in the direction of the light and God's grace makes this partnership itself a possibility.

Convincing grace brings us to the threshold of conversion. Wesley connects grace in this sense with repentance. Whenever we stand in the presence of God, we are convicted about how far we are from what God intends us to be. With God's light shining upon us and into our hearts, we realize, like the prodigal son in Jesus' parable (Luke 15:11-32), just how far we are from home. "Salvation is carried on by 'convincing grace,'" claims Wesley, "usually in scripture termed 'repentance,' which brings a larger measure of self-knowledge and a farther deliverance from the heart of stone."[12]

In his sermon on "The Way to the Kingdom," John addresses the human condition and the need we have for God to turn us around:

> Repent, that is, know yourselves. This is the first repentance, previous to faith, even conviction or self-knowledge. Awake, then, you who are sleeping. . . . The eyes of your understanding are darkened so that they cannot discern God or the things of God. The clouds of ignorance and error rest upon you and cover you with the shadow of death. You know nothing yet as you ought to know, neither God, nor the world, nor yourself. Your will is no longer the will of God. . . there is no soundness in your soul.[13]

Repentance is the first great movement, therefore, of the way of salvation. The Greek word in the New Testament from which this term comes, means "to be turned around." The same word can be translated "conversion."

Repentance alters the course of our lives. This turning is God's action upon us, but it cannot be achieved unless we are fully involved. Repentance reveals both what we need to be saved *from* and what we

12. Wesley, *Works*, 3:203.
13. Wesley, *Works*, 1:225–26.

need to be saved *into*. For the Wesleys, salvation is related both to Christ's redemptive work *for* us and the Spirit's transforming work *in* us. It revolves around freedom from sin and freedom to love. Repentance, therefore, is like the threshold of a door that opens the way to our spiritual healing. It is like the first step in the journey that leads us home.

Justifying grace, John Wesley says, is like the door itself leading into the home. Through justifying grace God does for us what we could never accomplish in our own right. The Wesleys believed that, through this work of grace, God simultaneously transforms us inwardly and outwardly. The outward experience they call justification, God's declaration of our righteousness in Christ. To use the forensic language of the courtroom, we are judged "not guilty" despite our broken state. But the wonder of God's grace does not stop here because the Wesleys could not imagine God would declare us righteous (wonderful as that is) without going on to make us so.

Simultaneous with this outward change, therefore, inwardly God regenerates the soul. God not only wants us to be declared godly and true, despite the fact we fail in that regard; God created us to love, so God launches us on our journey to that goal in this experience of grace. God not only imputes Christ's righteousness to us; God imparts goodness, beauty, and love through the presence of the indwelling Spirit. As a consequence of this real change, Christ abides in us and we in him—the life of God in the human soul which Jesus described in John 15.[14] This "new birth" (John 3:3-21) enables us to see and enter the kingdom of God. This use of "birth" language with regard to this activity of grace in our lives signals to us that conversion is only the beginning of our journey and not its end. The Wesleys declared the same.

That inward change also signals God's work of *sanctifying grace*. John Wesley described conversion as "sanctification begun" (as a way of weaving the singular tapestry of saving grace). The goal toward which this grace leads he conceived as *theosis*. This idea of "Christian

14. It is worth noting here that John 15 was the biblical basis for the Covenant Renewal Service in early Methodism, the Wesleys' testimony to the ongoing nature of conversion (i.e., increasing conformity to Christ) and our need to regularly recommit ourselves to the vine-branch relationship.

perfection" or "perfect love" he drew from Eastern more than Western Christianity. It affirms the extensiveness (depth and breadth) of grace to transform us. We will write more about this in the conversation about sustenance that follows here immediately. For the moment, suffice it to say that sanctifying grace saves us to the uttermost. It is God's loving act to bring us into increasing conformity to Christ, summed up as the life of holy love.

And that brings us to *glorifying grace*. While focusing on the eschatological dimensions of grace, John Wesley saw it in relation to the growth in grace which precedes our death. Before we die, we mature from one degree of glory to another (2 Cor 3:18). He described this as an experience in which "we fix the eye of our mind more and more steadfastly on his glory displayed in the gospel."[15] The movement from earth to heaven is a trajectory begun through sanctifying grace.[16] Life in time is part of life in eternity. The trajectory of the way of salvation is begun before we die, leading us into its glorious consummation, its *telos*.[17] We will develop this more in the conversation about restoration.

Third, *there are two initial responses to God's love and grace*. What are the effects of this redeeming grace—this way of salvation—upon us? God's grace cannot be fully realized, given its relational character, apart from our response to it. Wesleyan theology is, by definition, a theology of participation. St. Paul develops this concept in relation to Holy Communion, in particular, as a participation in the body and blood of Christ (1 Cor 10:16). Participation, that's the word. The Wesleys understand faith precisely in this way. In the rest of this conversation, and the next two, we will unpack salient features of our participation, of our response to grace, our "yes" to the "Divine Yes."[18]

Awakening is our first response to God's grace in our lives. God speaks and shows, and that revelation stirs us out of a spiritual slumber.

---

15. Wesley, *New Testament Notes*, comment on 2 Cor 3:18.
16. Maddox, *Responsible Grace*, 191.
17. Williams, *John Wesley's Theology Today*, 191.
18. E. Stanley Jones's final book, *The Divine Yes* (Nashville: Abingdon Press, 1975) is a powerful testimony to the objective and subjective dimensions of grace.

Charles Wesley entitled one of his moving sermons "Awake Thou That Sleepest."[19] Based upon St. Paul's words, "Wake up, sleeper! Get up from the dead, and Christ will shine on you" (Eph 5:14), he emphasized that our natural state (with all of its assets) is not the fullness of what God intends for us. So, as we have seen, through prevenient grace, God initiates the process of redemption in ways that rouse us from insensibility. We awaken out of "unreality" into "Reality," manifesting what John Wesley called our "first wish to please God."[20]

With respect to this essential response to God, the Wesleys align themselves, not only with the classical Christian tradition, but also with the great world's religions. Richard Rohr has captured the universality of awakening: "Great religion seeks utter awareness and full consciousness, so that we can, in fact, receive all. Everything belongs and everything can be received."[21] This idea of full consciousness that gives rise to receptivity resonates well with Wesleyan theology. Jesus simply described this as "having eyes that see" (Mark 8:18). Awakening is our first response to grace. Within the Wesleyan tradition, it is part of the way of salvation because it launches our desire to, as Paul put it, "carry out your own salvation within fear and trembling" (Phil 2:12). And even the desire to do this is a gift of God's grace.[22]

We awaken to the wonder of creation, our place in it as God's beloved, and to a living hope that God "who started a good work in you will stay with you to complete the job by the day of Christ Jesus" (Phil 1:6). For this very reason the note of joy sounds forth in our response to God. It really is amazing grace. Awakening is our "yes" to God's invitation to live abundantly. This awakening—true self-knowledge or repentance in the Wesleyan tradition—reflects an enlarged mind (*metanoia*). It moves us to look at life in a new way. This "change of

19. Wesley, *Works*, 1:142–58.

20. Wesley, *Works*, 3:203.

21. Richard Rohr, *Essential Teachings on Love* (Maryknoll: Orbis Books, 2018), 34.

22. In this sense, there is no such thing as natural free will. Our capacity to desire to live for God is itself a gift of God's prevenient grace, which prevented the loss of our will in the fall. By God's grace, we have eyes to see!

heart (and consequently of life) from all sin to all holiness," as Wesley concludes from Luke 3:8, provides a new perspective on life in general and our lives in particular.[23] Using the word "all" twice, Wesley points to the ultimate nature of the transformation that begins in our awakening. He describes repentance as "the necessary preparation for that inward kingdom."[24]

On God's side of this interrelationship, this hardly means cheap grace, as the cross forever reminds us. And from our side, awakening seldom comes quickly and easily. It occurs in liminal space in an experience of disorder.[25] Awakening is an in-between time when we must leave the known for the unknown (see Gen 12:1). This includes letting the old pass away so that the new can come (2 Cor 5:17). James Fowler identified this in John Wesley's faith development between 1725–1738, an extended period of leaving the "conventional stage" and moving into the "reflective stage"—a time when he had to attain a more personal and a less institutional (family and church) identity.[26]

Attachment is our second response to God's grace in our lives. Convincing grace convicts us, like the prodigal, of our failure (negatively) and our freedom (positively) as God's children. In light of this self-awareness and the revelation of God's unconditional love nonetheless in Christ, we throw ourselves into his arms. We stake our lives on Jesus. We attach to Christ in two fundamental ways: commitment and congruence. Commitment is a multi-faceted adherence to historic Christianity with an accompanying personal investment of ourselves in that faith as a living sacrifice (Rom 12:1). As important as it is to believe in certain things (the so-called substance of faith), the Wesleys

23. Wesley, *New Testament Notes*, comments on Luke 3:8.

24. Wesley, *New Testament Notes*, comments on Matt 3:2 and 4:17.

25. Richard Rohr, *The Wisdom Pattern: Order, Disorder, Reorder* (Cincinnati: Franciscan Media, 2020) looks at the transformative process as a movement from order, through disorder, to reorder.

26. James W. Fowler, "John Wesley's Development in Faith," an unpublished and undated article that applied his stages-of-faith typology to John Wesley's life; cf. his book, *Stages of Faith: The Psychology of Human Development and the Quest for Meaning* (New York: HarperCollins, 1981). Wesley's diary and published journal provide his own accounts of this awakening.

point to the act of faith, or that living faith by which one believes, as the foundation of the Christian life. *The* faith must become, at some point and in a dynamic way, *my* faith. Commitment reflects this kind of faith.

As St. Paul describes it, our investment is twofold. On the one hand, we cease being conformed to the patterns of the world (materialism, hedonism, and power) and instead seek transformation by the renewing of our minds. Our outlook on life is radically different, igniting a new way of living. In his hymn "And Can It Be?" Charles Wesley put this idea into poetry. Spiritual liberation—"My chains fell off, my heart was free"—Charles links with spiritual commitment—"I rose, went forth, and followed thee."[27] Commitment in the Wesleyan tradition is lived theology, beliefs turned into behaviors.

Dallas Willard offers a transformative understanding of commitment in his book *The Divine Conspiracy*.[28] He shows the insufficiency of both a "conversion mentality" (i.e., new birth as the goal) and a "membership mentality" (i.e., institutional affiliation as the goal). Rather, he commends a "discipleship mentality" as the gospel energy that ignites the flame of the Christian life. He roots discipleship in Jesus' message of the kingdom of God with a focus on the Sermon on the Mount. The Wesleys would celebrate his view.[29]

This energy ignites congruence, our desire to become increasingly like Christ. The Wesleys would like the contemporary description of Jesus as the Human One. Jesus demonstrates what true humanity looks like. The Incarnation, in and of itself, provides a paradigm for us to follow—an invitation to a way of living that is attainable by grace. Jesus is the Christian's pattern.[30] Inwardly we grow into his likeness in our character; outwardly we manifest his image in conduct. This is the

27. Wesley, *Hymns and Sacred Poems* (1739), 118.

28. Dallas Willard, *The Divine Conspiracy: Rediscovering Our Hidden Life in God* (New York: HarperCollins, 1998).

29. Thirteen of John Wesley's fifty-two Standard Sermons are based on Jesus' sermon on the mount.

30. The term "Christian pattern" was the title John Wesley chose when he published an abridgement of Thomas à Kempis's classic, *The Imitation of Christ*. See Conversation 2 above.

congruence (inward/outward) of life which commences when we attach ourselves to Christ. "The Christian life," so claims Eugene Peterson, "is the lifelong practice of attending to the details of congruence."[31] He describes this as "a long obedience in the same direction."[32] The Wesleys called this "going on to perfection"—that is, living day after day in ways that increase our conformity to Christ.

Early in the Methodist movement, John Wesley used the metaphor of a house to depict the flow of grace. Repentance is the porch. Faith is the door. Holiness is the interior of the house itself.[33] Awakening (repentance) and attachment (faith) get us onto the porch and through the door into the wonder of redemption. In the next two conversations, we look at how we move into our true home and experience the fullness of faith.

31. Eugene Peterson, *Christ Plays in Ten Thousand Places* (Grand Rapids: Eerdmans, 2005), 333.

32. See Eugene Peterson, *A Long Obedience in the Same Direction: Discipleship in an Instant Society* (Downers Grove, IL: InterVarsity Press, 1980).

33. See Wesley, *Works*, 9:227.

Reflection Questions

Conversation 6 (Redemption)

1. What part of this Conversation spoke most to you? Why is it important for you to hear this right now?

2. Remembering that the flow of grace is cyclical, not just sequential, where do you sense you are awakening to new things these days? Where are you attaching yourself more firmly? Where are you advancing in the life of faith?

3. How do you give thanks to God for redeeming you along the lines noted in this Conversation?

Conversation 7

The Delight of Sustenance

Brother Mark Gibbard, SSJE used to travel to Africa frequently. He loved talking about preparations for a safari. Paul had a conversation with him at St. Paul's United Theological College in Limuru, Kenya, a part of which went something like this.

"The safari," he said, "is a journey that requires preparation, wonder, and reflection. But the most important parts of the safari relate to the front-end preparations and the after-glow reflections."

"What do you make provision for a safari?" I asked.

"Well, it's all about basics. You need the necessities. You must take the right kinds of food for the duration of the trip. You need clothing that fits the climate and your surroundings. You need to be physically ready and also mentally and spiritually prepared."

"Why is spiritual preparation required?"

"Every journey you take is a trip into your inner self and an opportunity to reflect on your relationship with the God who is always with you," he advised. "It's an opportunity to encounter God anew and discover important things about yourself. If you have not made provision for the trip, your attention gets diverted from these really important things."

"So you're saying essentially that a safari is not simple," I observed wryly.

"Absolutely. The safari has a beginning, a middle, and an end. You need to be well-prepared for each phase. Sustenance is the key. Without proper provision and all you need to sustain you in the journey, you can't grow through it."

In the last conversation we looked at the beginning stages of entering your true home, to continue John Wesley's metaphor. The porch represents awakening, defined by the Wesleys as repentance. The door signifies attachment, the experience of justification by grace through faith, or simply faith. As we make our way through the doorway, we are poised to enter the house and explore its rooms for the rest of our lives. As we do so, we respond to sanctifying grace. Our deepest growth in grace takes place here as God's love works in our lives in a sustained way, as we grow into deeper levels of personal and social holiness. We engage ourselves for the long-haul.

Interestingly, Isaiah described this kind of spiritual engagement using the imagery of paths and streams (Isa 43:19). The Hebrew word in the verse can be translated both ways, and this is an intriguing idea. It is a way of reminding ourselves that our life in God is both a journey and a provision, a following and a feeding, guidance and nourishment, a path and a stream. The Wesleys certainly saw it this way. Charles Wesley drew upon this same imagery as he celebrated God as Creator and Provider:

Author of every work divine,
You, who through both creations shine,
The God of nature and of grace,
Your glorious steps in all we view,
And wisdom celebrate in you,
And power, and majesty, and praise.

Thou dost create the earth anew,
(Its Maker and Preserver too)
By thine almighty arm sustain;
Nature perceives thy secret force,
And still holds on her even course,
And owns thy providential reign.

Thou art the universal soul,
The plastic power that fills the whole,

And governs earth, air, sea, and sky,
The creatures all, thy breath receive,
And who by thy inspiring live,
Without thy inspiration die.

Spirit immense, eternal mind,
Thou on the souls of lost mankind
Dost with benignest influence move,
Pleased to restore the ruined race,
And new-create a world of grace
In all the image of thy love.[1]

First, *Wesleyan formation is a journey into holiness*. The Wesleys call this journey, this path, this river of life, sanctification or the quest for holiness. Through this process God conforms us increasingly to Christ in our living and restores the loving *imago Christi* in our lives. This journey requires ongoing sustenance. The theme of holiness ran through the life of John Wesley as a continuous stream from beginning to end and became one of the most significant marks of Methodism.[2] He claimed that this message of sanctifying grace and the goal of perfect love was "the grand depositum" of Methodism, the chief reason God raised up the people called Methodists.[3] This was his assessment of the Methodist movement just six months before his death. It was the vision that fueled his ministry for decades, and the one he hoped would continue to ignite future Methodists.

The irony is that Methodism's grand depositum has become its great debate, to the extent that Methodist preachers omit or minimize preaching and teaching on sanctification. Sadly, the theology of

---

1. John and Charles Wesley, *Hymns of Petition and Thanksgiving for the Promise of Father* (Bristol: Farley, 1746), 31–32. Modernized text.

2. See John Wesley, *The Works of John Wesley, Volume 13, Doctrinal and Controversial Treatises II*, ed. Paul W. Chilcote and Kenneth J. Collins (Nashville: Abingdon Press, 2013), 3–25, for an extensive introduction to Wesley's many publications on this theme—Christian perfection.

3. John Wesley, *The Letters of the Rev. John Wesley, A.M. Volume 8*, ed. John Telford, 238. Letter dated September 15, 1790.

"perfect love" has either become passé or a place of mean-spiritedness in the Wesleyan family. We believe this is a fundamental problem that robs the Wesleyan way of its greatest light and life—what the Wesleys described as "the fullness of faith." We see the loss largely created by an argument over how sanctification occurs (whether through crisis or process), and we believe the needed recovery of this central message will not occur if we keep debating this.

Rather, we see the recovery coming through a proclamation of God's provision for us throughout the journey into deeper love. This puts the emphasis on God's presence and purpose, shifting it away from our human efforts and achievements in the direction of perfection. We summarize this gracious activity in the term "sustenance." To say it another way, after our conversion, God continues to give us our meat and drink for abundant living. We do not live on provisions from the past. "Now is the day of salvation" (2 Cor 6:2), and like the manna in the wilderness, God's faithful love and compassion "are renewed every morning" (Lam 3:23).

In his sermon *On Zeal*, John Wesley paints a helpful word picture of the sustained Christian life.[4] He portrays living the Wesleyan way as concentric circles revolving around the love of Christ enthroned upon the human heart. Closest to the center are the fruits of the Spirit, shaped both by works of mercy and piety, all practiced within the context of the community of faith. You will find no better explanation of how God nourishes us in our journey to holiness of heart and life.

Second, counterintuitively, ***sustenance includes our abandonment to God.*** St. Paul describes the kind of abandonment we mean in Philippians 2:5-11. Often referred to as having "the mind of Christ," our imitation of Christ, in this regard, includes assuming the disposition or inclination of heart that enabled him to be faithful to God's will. As we have already seen (see Conversation 2 on humility), the Wesleys developed their theology around the classical idea of ***kenosis*** from the hymn quoted by Paul. Eastern Christian spirituality—a critical source for the Wesleys' vision—emphasized the self-emptied Christ who seeks

4. See Wesley, *Works*, 3:313–14.

a union (oneness) with God expressed in daily living.[5] Jesus understood his relationship with God in this way: "I and the Father are one" (John 14:30), a union that generated a radical dependency. "The Son can do nothing by himself, but only what he sees the Father doing" (John 5:19). Only face-to-face attentiveness can lead to this kind of sight. A literal rendering of the Greek text—"The Word was facing God" (John 1:1)—reveals a posture or disposition which Jesus continued in the Incarnation (see Luke 5:16).

Elaine Heath has written helpfully about *kenosis*, showing how it is the way God calls us to live, and through the Spirit gives us the grace to do so. She calls kenosis "the profound paradigm shift" that occurs in us when we realize that God, not our experience of God, is the focus of holiness.[6] This keeps the source and authority of our faith and practice precisely where it belongs. But it also keeps the substance of love paramount, for God is love. Indeed, the mind of Christ is the attitude and action of love.[7]

The kenotic pattern seen in Christ is one God effects in us by virtue of our abandonment. It cultivates the same qualities we see in him: humility, renunciation, servanthood, obedience, and sacrifice. All these qualities give evidence of our love of God and others. Thomas Jay Oord sums up the primacy of love in abandonment in a simple phrase: "Jesus' life reveals that God always loves."[8] Having the mind of Christ means that we love always too. These descriptions are Wesleyan theology writ large. Abandonment is the essence of our sustenance, in both a moment of surrender and the ongoing process which follows it. The Wesleys used an equally pithy statement to make this point. It is the opening line of the prayer for covenant renewal: "I am no longer

5. Kallistos Ware, *The Orthodox Way*, rev. ed. (Yonkers, NY: St. Vladimir's Seminary Press, 2012). This survey sheds light on where and how the Wesleys drew from this tradition to see theology as a way of faith and life.

6. Elaine Heath, *The Mystic Way of Evangelism* (Grand Rapids: Baker Academic, 2008), 66.

7. Dennis F. Kinlaw, *The Mind of Christ* (Grand Rapids: Francis Asbury Press, 1998), offers a good study of kenosis.

8. Thomas J. Oord, *Pluriform Love*, 160.

my own, but thine."[9] Our sustenance begins in our renunciation of egotism and ethnocentrism, and in our reliance on God.

Third, *abiding in Christ sustains our journey.* Jesus taught this in John 15. St. Paul summed it up in two words—"in Christ"—a phrase he used more frequently than any other in his writings. Not surprisingly, John Wesley made John 15 the biblical reading for the annual Covenant Renewal Service. And he made Galatians 2:20 a hallmark verse for understanding the sanctified life, calling the indwelling Christ "a fountain of life in my inmost soul, from which all my tempers, words and actions flow."[10] From these passages, and others like them, the Wesleys understood abiding in Christ as living and growing in love. Increase of love toward God and others defines the sanctified life. Love is the path and the provision. Living in Christ and immersing ourselves in God's grace sustain the journey.

Given the fact that we need grace to mature or grow in our faith, is should not surprise us that the "means of grace" figure prominently in the Wesleyan understanding of discipleship. The instituted means (works of piety) and the prudential means (works of mercy) are the usual channels through which God enables us to "bear much fruit" (John 15:5).[11] Practicing these spiritual disciplines is one of the most critical ways that we abide in Christ. John Wesley makes this clear in one of his best-known sermons, "The Means of Grace."[12] He describes there how the means play a critical role in our spiritual growth and how, as an expression of sanctifying grace, they enable heart-renewal in the image of God.

John Wesley identified five instituted means of grace: prayer, fasting, searching the scriptures, the Lord's Supper, and Christian

---

9. *United Methodist Hymnal*, 607.

10. Wesley, *New Testament Notes*, comment on Gal 2:20.

11. Henry H. Knight III, *The Presence of God in the Christian Life: John Wesley and the Means of Grace* (Metuchen, NJ: Scarecrow Press, 1992) remains one of the most extensive studies of the means of grace. Elaine Heath's book, *Five Means of Grace: Experience God's Love the Wesleyan Way* (Nashville: Abingdon Press, 2017), is an excellent study of the instituted means of grace, useful for group study.

12. Wesley, *Works*, 1:376–97.

conferencing.[13] Charles Wesley celebrates them all in a single stanza of a hymn:

> The prayer, the fast, the word conveys,
> When mixt with faith, thy life to me,
> In all the channels of thy grace,
> I still have fellowship with thee,
> But chiefly here my soul is fed
> With fullness of immortal bread.[14]

These works of piety help to form the life of inward holiness.

The Wesleys define works of mercy more by their intention—that is, they include everything we say and do for the good of others. Obviously, there are many ways to do this. To provide specific examples, John Wesley cites feeding the hungry, clothing the naked, assisting the stranger, visiting those who are sick or imprisoned, comforting the afflicted, instructing the ignorant, reproving the wicked, encouraging those who do good, and giving generously to the poor.[15] Taken together, the means of grace are the practices through which we enact the two great commandments.

Much has been written about the various means of grace in the Wesleyan tradition. But given the centrality of Eucharist in the faith and practice of the Wesleys, we want to focus on this meal for just a moment. In this great sign-act of God's love we see important patterns for living the Wesleyan way. The four-fold action of Eucharist provides a paradigm for our life journey with and to God. As we repeatedly participate in the eucharistic actions of taking, blessing, breaking, and giving—the constitutive elements of an authentic,

13. See Steve Harper, *Devotional Life in the Wesleyan Tradition: A Workbook* (Nashville: Upper Room, 1995); cf. Elaine Heath, *Five Means of Grace: Experience God's Love the Wesleyan Way*, and Paul W. Chilcote, ed., *The Wesleyan Tradition: A Paradigm for Renewal* (Nashville: Abingdon Press, 2002), 87–97.

14. Wesley, *Hymns on the Lord's Supper*, 39.

15. See Chilcote, *The Wesleyan Tradition*, 98–110; cf. Theodore Jennings Jr. *Good News to the Poor* (Nashville: Abingdon Press, 1990).

Christian life—God conforms us to the image of Christ.[16] Our lives become truly eucharistic as faith working by love leads to holiness of heart and life. Other patterns related to the meal inspire us with wonder as well. As in all worship, God descends in order that we might ascend—we lift up our hearts to God. God reveals God's self in the meal and we respond by offering God's life of love to the world. We come into the presence of Christ at the table and are sent by him into the world. As we regularly participate in the Lord's Supper, we are increasingly formed into the image of Christ and sent forth in his name to love and serve others.

Fourth, *associating with companions enhances our wonder.* One of the other instituted means of grace—Christian fellowship or conference—merits separate discussion and a major point of its own related to sustenance. Fellowship in small groups was the heartbeat of Methodism. We need each other. It is that simple. But our need is also a profound gift. On its most basic level, the purpose of fellowship in the early Methodist Societies was simply richer communion with God through Christ. But companionship with others enhanced the sense of wonder in life for the early Methodists. That word, "companion," literally means "to share one's bread." Methodist people from the very beginning have sustained one another by their presence, understanding, empathy, and support. In this respect the Wesleys surely understood themselves to be spiritual guides.[17]

In defense of his expanding movement of spiritual renewal, John Wesley declares the rediscovery of mutual accountability in fellowship as the critical and distinguishing mark of the movement: "We introduce Christian fellowship where it was utterly destroyed," he claims. "And the fruits of it have been peace, joy, love, and zeal for every good word

---

16. See Paul W. Chilcote, "Eucharist and Formation," in *Theology, Eucharist and Ministry: Wesleyan Perspectives,* ed. Jason E. Vickers, pp. 183–201 (Nashville: General Board of Higher Education and Ministry, 2016); cf. Henri Nouwen, *Life of the Beloved* (New York: Crossroad, 1992), in which he shows how this pattern stands at the heart of the spiritual life.

17. See Steve Harper, "John Wesley: Spiritual Guide," *Wesleyan Theological Journal* 20, 2 (Fall 1985): 93–98.

and work."[18] He attempted to provide all the necessary elements for genuine *koinonia*—community. He knew that we bear fruit when our many branches are intertwined with Christ (John 15). A robust ecclesiology characterizes Methodist theology, a vision of the church as community in which Christ is "the only foundation."[19] The purpose of Christian fellowship, however, is not be found in the church itself, but in the church's ministry in the world—in good works that demonstrate God's love for all.

Fifth, *those sustained by God abound in good works.* Shaped by abandonment to God, abiding in Christ, and associating with others in matters of faith and practice, the Wesleys believed that Christians would abound in good works. Agreeing with James that "faith without actions is dead" (James 2:26), they called faith without works "that grand pest of Christianity."[20] Wherever this takes root, John argues, it fills the church with "envy, strife, confusion, and every evil work." His words and insights are much needed in the church today. We need a revival of faith-inspired works, a movement of renewal that attends to the wellness of fellow Christians and then embraces the whole world. Faith and works, inward and outward holiness simply must be held together. A contemporary concept helps explain how seemingly opposite aspects of life, like these, work together. The term for this is "nondual consciousness."[21] The Wesleys were expert in this, and we must be in the living of our faith today.

Nondual consciousness can be seen particularly in the way the Wesleys held together inward and outward holiness. John actually defined Methodists using these nondual images. "By Methodists," he declares in his *Advice to the People Called Methodists*, "I mean a people who profess to pursue (in whatsoever measure they have attained)

18. John Wesley, *The Works of the Rev. John Wesley, A.M.*, ed. Thomas Jackson, 14 vols., reprint ed. (Grand Rapids: Zondervan, 1958), 8:347.

19. Wesley, *New Testament Notes*, comment on Matt 16:18.

20. Wesley, *Works*, 2:459.

21. Richard Rohr, *The Naked Now* (New York: Crossroad, 2009). Cynthia Bourgeault, *The Heart of Centering Prayer: Nondual Christianity in Theory and Practice* (Boston: Shambhala, 2016).

holiness of heart and life, inward and outward conformity in all things to the revealed will of God. . . . universal love filling the heart and governing the life."[22] In his sermon on "The End of Christ's Coming," he articulates this essential synthesis: "O do not take anything less than this for the religion of Jesus Christ! Do not take part of it for the whole. What God has joined together, put not asunder. Take no less for this religion than the 'faith that worketh by love', all inward and outward holiness."[23]

For the Wesleys, works are as important as faith and living in the world faithfully, and the community of faith plays an essential role in helping us live these out together. The quest for love in community results in a deeper and wider (panoramic) holiness than occurs when we separate the Christian life into pieces and parts. Living the Wesleyan way in community means doing so with the same intent as the first Christians in Jerusalem—namely, so none would be in need (Acts 2:44-45, 4:34). Commenting on this, John notes that their concern for one another was "the proof that great grace was upon them all," which he added was the natural fruit of love.[24]

Note the natural segway into the centrality of the fruit of the Spirit (Gal 5:22-23). John Wesley took the singularity of St. Paul's words to mean that love is the fruit, and "the root of all the rest."[25] The nine fruit combine the inward inclination of our hearts and the outward disposition of our wills. The fruit of the Spirit co-mingle character and conduct into a unified life of personal and social holiness—a life of faith working by love that results in watching over all in love. Charles Wesley packages this all potently in his lyrical reflection on the Galatians text:

> Jesus, plant thy Spirit in me,
> Then the fruit shall show the tree,
> Every grace its author prove,
> Rising from the root of love.

22. Wesley, *Works* (Jackson), 8:352.
23. Wesley, *Works*, 2:483.
24. Wesley, *New Testament Notes*, comment on Acts 4:34.
25. Wesley, *New Testament Notes*, comment on Gal 5:22.

Full of tenderness and care,
I shall every burden bear;
Glad the general servant be,
Serve with strict fidelity.[26]

The Wesleys believed that the Spirit distributes gifts to Christians who function as containers (ministers) in which the content (love) is carried and conveyed into the world. We believe that this unified work of the Spirit in and through us today provides the foundation for "a future filled with hope" (Jer 29:11).

The movement from abandonment to abounding is the journey (paths) and provision (streams) envisioned by Isaiah in 43:19. It is the vision enfleshed in Jesus, so that Christlikeness becomes the formative aim of theology. Sanctifying grace is a "going on to perfection" (*theosis*) in Christlikeness. Drawing from the wells of Eastern Orthodoxy, the Wesleys organized their theology and offered Christ with a vision of growth in grace as the maturation of love. We will say more about this in the next conversation. But everything we have said thus far confirms that the upward call is a wonder-full life. Yet, wonderful as it is up to this point, there is one further wave of grace to round out the picture of abundant living: glorifying grace. We explore it in the next conversation.

---

26. Wesley, *Scripture Hymns*, 2:309.

Reflection Questions

Conversation 7 (Sustenance)

1. What part of this Conversation spoke most to you? Why is it important for you to hear this right now?

2. Which of the means of grace do you most practice? Which of them do you need to improve?

3. How has life together in Christian community been helpful to you?

Conversation 8

The Glory of Restoration

On April 15, 2019 Notre Dame cathedral in Paris suffered a devastating fire. Questions about the viability of its repair were legitimately raised. Global sentiment to make the attempt, however, set in motion an immediate fund-raising effort, along with the gathering of an array of architects, engineers, artists, and construction workers to plan and carry out the project. Using some blueprints that go back to the cathedral's construction in 1163 CE, the restoration project will return the edifice to its previous glory, along with improvements that will protect it from vulnerability to a future fire.

The following excerpt is taken from an Overheard podcast in which Amy Briggs interviewed National Geographic photographer, Tomas Van Houtryve, who is developing a photographic history of the cathedral's restoration.[1]

Briggs: Since the fire, a massive restoration effort has been under way, exposing more than eight centuries of Notre Dame's history. In its long life, the cathedral has been damaged and repaired, re-envisioned and reconstructed, each time laying down a new layer to its story. And some of those layers are hundreds of years apart.

---

1. Overheard Podcast, Episode 1: Resurrecting Notre-Dame de Paris, January 18, 2022; https://www.nationalgeographic.com/podcasts/article/resurrecting-notre-dame-de-paris; accessed January 20, 2023. The half-hour broadcast is heavily and freely edited for our purposes here.

Van Houtryve: One of the things that keeps hitting me is the idea that the people that started building the cathedral knew it wouldn't be finished in their lifetime. And I can't really think of projects that we do today where we say we're going to start this and we're going to do it for four generations from now or five generations from now.

Briggs: So what are you hoping people take away from your work at Notre Dame?

Van Houtryve: I really think that we should reflect on this place and the role that it's had through time and culture and history. It's kind of one of these few projects on Earth that brings people together to make something that's more than the sum of its parts, that makes something kind of an incredible human creation that's still going on and moving forward toward a goal that we cannot even imagine.

Briggs: The devastating fire of 2019 may have added one more layer to the cathedral's ongoing evolution, but it won't be the last one. As so many who have dedicated themselves to this building have learned, they are part of its very long story. As we watch this restoration take place, we know that a new chapter of the cathedral's story is unfolding before our very eyes.

In this conversation we take a look together at God's ultimate goal of restoration. Our previous reflections on creation, redemption, and sustenance have all led us to this point. There is a certain sense in which our experience of wonder builds with each step of the way. Full restoration is the goal or *telos* of living the Wesleyan way. This is the whole point of it all. As we expound the wonder of restoration, let these words of St. Paul reverberate in your heart and your mind; "no eye has seen, nor ear heard, nor the human heart conceived, what God has prepared for those who love him" (1 Cor 2:9).

First, *God is at work restoring all things to their original glory*. John and Charles Wesley shared a "go to" text related to the process of restoration. "And all of us, with unveiled faces, seeing the glory of the Lord as though reflected in a mirror, are being transformed into the same image from one degree of glory to another" (2 Cor 3:18). In his lyrical paraphrase of this text in *Scripture Hymns*, Charles pleads:

Come then, and dwell in me,
Spirit of power within,
And bring the glorious liberty
From sorrow, fear, and sin:
The seed of sin's disease,
Spirit of health, remove,
Spirit of finished holiness,
Spirit of perfect love (*Scripture Hymns*, 2:298).

God, through the presence and power of the Holy Spirit, constantly strives to move us in the direction of "finished holiness" and "perfect love."

For the Wesleys, the biblical narrative moves from creation to new creation, a recapitulation of all things on earth and in heaven through Christ (Acts 3:21; Eph 1:9-10). God, as we have seen, created all things for goodness, beauty, and love. God works moment by moment to restore this wondrous trilogy of life to its original splendor. The restoration of which we speak is glorious. The Wesleys believed that a final wave of grace brings the restoration of all things in its wake. The concluding stanza of Charles's famous *Redemption Hymn*, "Love Divine, All Loves Excelling"—some of the most beloved lines in all his poetic production—celebrates this lofty goal:

Finish then thy new creation,
Pure and spotless let us be,
Let us see thy great salvation,
Perfectly restored in thee;
Changed from glory into glory,
Till in heaven we take our place,
Till we cast our crowns before thee,
Lost in wonder, love, and praise![2]

2. Wesley, *Redemption Hymns*, 12. Modernized text. The original of line two reads "sinless" rather than "spotless."

Second, *the process of restoration includes a "foretaste of glory divine."*[3] We capture glimpses of the "great salvation" here and there throughout the course of our lives. New creation breaks in, but we know that the culmination of all things will come only in its fullness in God's good time. To use the language of Charles Wesley, we "anticipate our heaven below."[4] He embedded that phrase in the final couplet of his hymn, "O for a thousand tongues to sing," but in a stanza seldom sung today. In his view, we await the new heaven and earth, "and own that love is heaven."[5] We experience heaven wherever love flourishes. S T Kimbrough, Jr. reminds us that Charles Wesley avoids restricting anticipation of heaven below "to our last gasp." "The spirit graciously transforms us in progressive degrees," according to Wesley, "with perfection as the 'last degree.'"[6]

Colin Williams put it this way, "It is apparent that Wesley's eschatology has a great deal to do with his view of the way the Christian lives now."[7] We have observed that John Wesley's sermons often conclude with an appeal, claiming that whatever you have heard him say, you can experience today. "Today is the day of salvation" (2 Cor 6:2) served as the keynote of his preaching. He encouraged the Methodists to look actively for God's reign shining through the darkness. These "first fruits" encourage us in the journey. "The kingdom of heaven and the kingdom of God," he maintained, "are but two phrases for the same thing. They mean, not barely a future happy state in heaven, but

3. This phrase comes, not from Charles Wesley, but from another great Methodist hymn writer, Fanny Crosby, and her hymn "Blessed Assurance," in particular. See Paul W. Chilcote, *Singing the Faith: Soundings of Lyrical Theology in the Methodist Tradition* (Nashville: Wesley's Foundery Books, 2020), 48–55.

4. See Randy L. Maddox, "'Anticipate Our Heaven Below': The Emphatic Hope and Abiding Tone of Charles Wesley's Eschatology," *Proceedings of the Charles Wesley Society* 17 (2013): 11–34.

5. Wesley, *Works*, 7:79. Although Charles Wesley wrote this hymn in 1739, it was not published until 1780.

6. S T Kimbrough Jr., "Charles Wesley and the Journey of Sanctification," *Evangelical Journal* 16 (1998): 49–75.

7. Williams, *Wesley's Theology for Today*, 191.

a state to be enjoyed on earth."[8] For him, holiness equals happiness. Seize the day, therefore, even as you await the ultimate day of God's victory in love. Joy characterizes our earthly life in Christ; we can only anticipate the joy of the new creation yet to come.

Third, *God seeks to restore all people to the uttermost.* In British Methodism, Wesleyan theology is often summarized by what are known as the "four alls." All people need to be saved. All people can be saved. All people can know they are saved. All people can be saved to the uttermost. We broached this fourth "all" in the previous conversation by alluding to the idea of *theosis*. As we continue to think about restoration, we need to expand your understanding of this vision and what it implies. It begs the question, Just how far can we actually advance in Christlikeness?

The Wesleys took their cue in this regard from the Bible. "Dear friends, now we are God's children," St. John observes, "and it hasn't yet appeared what we will be. We know that when he appears we will be like him because we will see him as he is" (1 John 3:2). If John Wesley were to define *theosis*, he might easily say that it is "the glory of God penetrating our inmost substance."[9] He developed this idea drawing largely on the Eastern Orthodox tradition, where the concept of Christian perfection is ongoing (perfecting) rather than completed (perfected). In the Orthodox tradition, moreover, *theosis* means the maturing or fullness of love in and through us.[10] Undoubtedly, both traditions draw this concept of ever-expanding love from St. Paul who said that "when the perfect comes, what is partial will be brought to an end" (1 Cor 13:10).

Orthodox theologian Peter Bouteneff finds resonance between the Wesleys and his own tradition around the "themes of salvation as

8. Wesley, *New Testament Notes*, comment on Matt 3:2.

9. Wesley, *New Testament Notes*, comment on 1 John 3:2.

10. Michael J. Christiansen, "The Royal Way of Love: Deification in the Wesleyan Tradition," in *With All the Fullness of God*, ed. Jared Ortiz, 177–202 (London: Lexington Books, 2021).

restoration, and as change and movement from glory to glory."[11] Not only the idea of salvation as restoration, but also the Pauline concept of "participation," unites these two great traditions. S T Kimbrough Jr. defines *theosis*, in fact, as participation in the divine nature.[12] He illustrates this connection with an example from Wesley's *Nativity Hymns* in which the twin themes of Incarnation and restoration find profound expression:

> Made flesh for our sake,
> That we might partake
> The nature divine,
> And again in his image, his holiness shine;
>
> And while we are here,
> Our King shall appear,
> His Spirit impart,
> And form his full image of love in our heart.[13]

God's restoration as *theosis* brings far more than external conformity to law. This is the danger of many Methodists today who define holiness in terms of obedience to the law of God. Rather, *theosis* means a renewal of the heart in love—a participation in God's love that leads to love of God and love of others.[14] Restoring grace begins in prevenient grace and reaches its fullness in glorifying grace—all because of love.[15]

---

11. Peter Bouteneff, "All Creation in United Thanksgiving: Gregory of Nyssa and the Wesleys on Salvation," in *Orthodox and Wesleyan Spirituality*, ed. S T Kimbrough, Jr. (Crestwood, NY: St. Vladimir's Seminary Press, 2002), 194.

12. S T Kimbrough, Jr., *The Lyrical Theology of Charles Wesley: A Reader* (Eugene, OR: Wipf & Stock, 2011), 89.

13. Charles Wesley, *Hymns for the Nativity of our Lord* (London: Strahan, 1745), 12.

14. See Harold Mayo, "John Wesley and the Christian East: On the Subject of Christian Perfection" (Crestwood, NY: St. Vladimir's Orthodox Theological Seminary, Master's thesis, 1980); cf. Randy L. Maddox, "John Wesley and Eastern Orthodoxy: Influences, Convergences, and Differences," *Asbury Theological Journal* 45, 2 (1990): 29–53

15. See Maddox, *Responsible Grace*, 106–9.

Fourth, *God intends universal flourishing for the whole creation.* Like St. Paul, John and Charles Wesley's vision of salvation is social and cosmic, not simply personal. Most certainly, to paraphrase Irenaeus of Lyons, the greatest glory of God is the human being fully alive. But the biblical vision of salvation as restoration goes far beyond the redemption of individuals. God desires and intends universal flourishing. For our purposes here, this question begs two important questions. Will God's desire be realized in the life of every human being? What does God's intention imply with regards to the whole creation?

The first question raises the perennial issue of universalism. Does the Wesleyan view of unlimited atonement and saving grace offered to all imply that all will be saved? The Wesleys affirmed St. Paul's words, "The love of Christ controls us, because we have concluded this: one died for the sake of all" (2 Cor 5:14). The "all" for Paul means all. It does for the Wesleys too. They lived in the light of 2 Peter 3:9, with God, "not wanting anyone to perish, but all to change their hearts and lives." If God's restorative salvation is universal in its purpose, how far does it go in its realization?

Seeking a response to these questions leaves us wishing we could sit down with John and Charles and ask them outright. We are left, however, to pour over their works and do our best to interpret them. We have done that and the message, unfortunately, is neither definitive nor singular. On the one hand, we encounter a traditional theology of eternity, with heaven and hell in full play forever.[16] But then in his sermon on "The General Deliverance" he leaves open the possibility that the entire creation will be restored—that God includes everyone and everything in the new creation.[17] He does not resolve this tension.

There is some evidence that John Wesley preferred to translate the Greek term *kolasin* as "correction" (discipline aimed to effect positive

16. See John Wesley's sermon "Of Hell" in *Works*, 3:30–44.
17. See his sermon "The General Deliverance" in *Works*, 2:436–50.

and redemptive change) rather than "punishment."[18] His comment on Ephesians 1:10 seems to affirm some form of universalism:

> That in the dispensation of the fullness of the times—In this last administration of God's fullest grace, which took place when the time appointed was fully come. He might gather together into one in Christ—might recapitulate, re-unite, and place in order again under Christ their common Head. ALL things which are in heaven, and on earth—ALL angels and men, whether living or dead, in the Lord.[19]

Clearly, the "last administration of God's fullest grace" is what we call glorifying grace, and the restoration it effects is universal. Likewise, in his comments on Acts 3:21 he affirms "the restitution of ALL things. . . . ALL Jews and Gentiles" (everyone, with "all" in bold caps to make the idea stand out) in an earthly union that has no signs of changing in eternity.[20] We cannot rule out God's judgment as an act of relentless mercy in which love wins.

One thing is abundantly clear. The Wesleys left the outworking of all this in the realm of mystery. Their theology of love left them satisfied with the view that God's judgment and mercy are in sync for our eternal good. What we can say with absolute confidence is that the Wesleys taught that Jesus' life, death, and resurrection create the *possibility* that all *may* be saved. They lived in the hope that love never fails. Moreover, the God they had come to know and love in Jesus desires union with all humanity. The purpose of creation was to celebrate relationships of love. God seeks the restoration of this goal above all things.

The second question about God's intention concerning the whole of creation requires less qualification. In an incisive article on "Salvation as Flourishing for the Whole Creation," Randy Maddox identifies three Wesleyan commitments that differentiate Methodism from other

---

18. See Maddox, *Responsible Grace*, 247–53 for a discussion of this complex issue.

19. Wesley, *New Testament Notes*, comment on Eph 1:10.

20. See similar sentiments expressed in "The Great Assize" in Wesley, *Works*, 1:353–75.

Christian traditions.[21] All three commitments reflect the conjunctive method in Wesleyan theology. Methodists anticipate the flourishing of bodies, not just souls; society, not just individuals; and creation, not just humans. God intends the restoration of all things, and here as elsewhere "all means all" for the Wesleys. Through grace, God leads all creation into a dance of joy, justice, and jubilee in which God's beloved children seek to radiate God's love, participate in God's reign, and seek the restoration of all things in the Three-One God.[22] At a time when this world—our earthly home—stands in such great peril, what a prophetic word this is to us. To be a follower of Jesus means to be faithful stewards of this fragile world and seek its full restoration.

Fifth, *the promise of New Creation is our basis for hope.* We are all in great need of hope today. John and Charles Wesley developed a theology characterized by an "optimism of grace." For them, the coalescence of faith, hope, and love generated this optimism—a Christian disposition akin to what some refer to as "positive psychology."[23] For the Wesleys, the three virtues arise, exist, and thrive in response to grace. Optimists assume the reality and potency of transformation and its value for all of life. The understanding that we are all God's beloved and that God seeks our fullest possible restoration—God wants you to flourish—produces a lot of hope. Wesley called this a "living hope."[24]

Hope leads ineluctably to the new creation; God's fullest possible restoration generates hope. Time moves into eternity and we respond joyfully and expectantly to grace as we live the Wesleyan way, confident that "the kingdom of the world has become the kingdom of our Lord and his Christ, and he will rule forever and always" (Rev 11:15). John

21. Randy L. Maddox, "Salvation as Flourishing for the Whole Creation: A Wesleyan Trajectory," in *Wesleyan Perspectives on Human Flourishing*, ed. Dean G. Smith and Rob A. Fringer, 1–23 (Eugene, OR: Pickwick, 2021).

22. Paul W. Chilcote, A *Faith That Sings: Biblical Themes in the Lyrical Theology of Charles Wesley* (Eugene, OR: Cascade Books, 2016), 9–13.

23. Positive psychology has matured into a discipline which has been beneficial to many, for which see Shane Lopez, Jennifer Teramoto Pedrotti, and C. R. Snyder, *Positive Psychology: The Scientific and Practical Explorations of Human Strengths* (Los Angeles: Sage Publications, 2019).

24. Wesley, *Works*, 13:142.

Wesley celebrated the fact that everything is now returning "to its rightful Master."[25] Through it all, God's grace predisposes our hearts toward the reconciliation and restoration realized in our lives and offered in and for our world.[26]

Professor Jürgen Moltmann—the father of the theology of hope—placed hope at the center of his theology.[27] In our book, *Living Hope*, we tell the story of how the seed of hope was planted in his life. It bears repeating here:

> During World War II there was a German prison of war camp on the northeast coast of England near the city of Hull. A young pastor and his wife served a small Methodist circuit close by. They were filled with compassion and compelled to do something to reach out to the German prisoners who were their neighbors. They went to the commander and asked permission to take a prisoner with them to church each Sunday and then to their home where they would eat their Sunday dinner together. It was agreed. Sunday after Sunday, a steady flow of German soldiers worshiped and ate with the Bakers in their home throughout the course of the war. This world-famous theologian paused, looked at Paul intently, and said, "One of those soldiers was a young man by the name of Jürgen Moltmann, and it was at Frank and Nellie Baker's dinner table that the seed of hope was planted in my heart." Hope is often fragile because life is fragile, but a simple act of kindness or hospitality can fan a flickering flame into a living hope.[28]

---

25. Wesley, *New Testament Notes*, comment on Rev 11:15.

26. See Paul Chilcote, "John and Charles Wesley on 'God in Christ Reconciling,'" *Methodist History*, 47, 3 (April 2009): 132–45.

27. His *Theology of Hope* (Minneapolis: Fortress Press, 1993) proved to be a watershed in contemporary theology, sounding anew the note of hope, his axial theme.

28. Paul W. Chilcote and Steve Harper, *A Living Hope: An Inclusive Vision of the Future* (Eugene: Cascade Books, 2019), 20–21. We were Prof. Baker's last two PhD students at Duke University. Nellie played a formative role in our lives and in the lives of our families during our time together. It is easy for us to see how Moltmann found hope in the Bakers. We did too.

Charles Wesley, like Moltmann and the Bakers, found hope in a meal. Nothing revealed the glory of restoration to him more than Jesus' portrait of the heavenly banquet, anticipated by us in the celebration of Holy Communion. This is a "soul-transporting feast," he sang, that "bears us now on eagles' wings" and "seals our eternal bliss."[29] In this eucharistic hymn he provides for us his own lyrical feast of participation, restoration, glory, and wonder:

How glorious is the life above
    Which in this ordinance we taste;
That fulness of celestial love,
    That joy which shall for ever last!

The light of life eternal darts
    Into our souls a dazzling ray,
A drop of heaven o'erflows our hearts,
    And deluges the house of clay.

Sure pledge of ecstasies unknown
    Shall this divine communion be,
The ray shall rise into a sun,
    The drop shall swell into a sea.[30]

29. Wesley, *Hymns on the Lord's Supper*, 82–83.
30. Wesley, *Hymns on the Lord's Supper*, 87.

Reflection Questions

Conversation 8 (Restoration)

1. Which part of this Conversation spoke most to you? Why is it important for you to hear this right now?

2. How does your vision of God's restoration influence your life now? How are you a co-creator with God?

3. What role does hope play in your spiritual formation?

MOVEMENT 3

The Way in and for the World

– Introduction –

Moving upward in Wesleyan formation positions us properly to receive God's gift of wisdom and opens our hearts and minds to the wonder that surrounds us and resides within us. But these discoveries are not simply for us, as if we possess them or use them for our exclusive benefit. John and Charles Wesley did not view their movement of spiritual renewal as something to hold onto tightly. Their ministry was more about opening doors than closing them, but then also caring intently about those who crossed that threshold into their Methodist home. Indeed, John and Charles Wesley did not believe their movement was about them. It was all about God and God's mission in and for the world. Our wisdom and even our wonder fail us if they leave us turned in on ourselves. We have received that others might taste and see that God is good (Psa 34:8).

In the so-called "Large Minutes" of the Methodist Conference, Wesley poses this question: "What may we reasonably believe to be God's design in raising up the preachers called 'Methodists'?" The answer was not "to help the lost secure a place in heaven." Nor was it the more lofty notion of enjoying the closest possible bonds of love with God in Christ. The answer: "To reform the nation, particularly the Church; and to spread scriptural holiness over the land."[1] Today we might say that the purpose was to partner with God in God's loving purposes, filling the world with God's love. As Methodists we are drawn to Christ so that God might spin us out into the world in

1. Wesley, *Works*, 10:845.

witness and service. Focused on ourselves, we die. When we partner with God in God's mission of love in and for the world, we come to life. This final movement explores that outflow. In some ways, this makes it more important than everything that has preceded. This is where it all becomes real.

The Wesleys built their theology and practice of a life in and for the world on their understanding of a Three-One God postured in perpetual, grace-filled, outward movement. "New every morning is your love, great God of light," we affirm in the Order for Morning Prayer and Praise in *The United Methodist Hymnal*, "and all day long you are working for good in the world."[2] God calls us to model that passion and that posture. Charles Wesley used a profound image to communicate this understanding of living in and for the world. He describes the authentic follower of Jesus as a "transcript of the Trinity." That means essentially that God writes God's self into our very being so that when other people "read" our lives, they perceive God in us:

Clothed with Christ, aspire to shine,
Radiance He of Light Divine;
Beam of the Eternal Beam,
He in God, and God in Him!
Strive we Him in Us to see,
Transcript of the Deity.[3]

John and Charles Wesley firmly believed that God was active and at work in the world to save and restore all creation. This primary conviction led them to reclaim mission as the church's reason for being.[4] They developed a holistic vision of faithful living that refused

2. *United Methodist Hymnal*, 877.

3. Wesley, *Hymns and Sacred Poems* (1739), 178.

4. The Wesleys poured enormous energy into the formation of authentic disciples of Jesus for the transformation of the world. Whereas words like "mission" and "evangelism" hardly ever appear in the Wesleyan corpus, the Wesleyan Revival was at once profoundly missional and evangelistic in nature. See David Bebbington, *Evangelicalism in Modern Britain: A History from the 1730s to the 1980s* (Grand Rapids: Baker Book House, 1989), 40.

to separate the gospel from the cultures in which it was immersed, the contemplative life from a life of action in the world, physical from spiritual needs, or the institutional church from the *missio Dei* in and for the world.

What does it mean, then, to live in and for the world in a Wesleyan way? In the early days of the Wesleyan revival, in 1742, John published a little tract entitled "The Character of a Methodist."[5] It had a very interesting subtitle: "Not as tho' I had already attained." It was an ideal portrait, in other words, a vision of what a Methodist could and should be and do. We want to offer you something like this through the four conversations that follow.

- First, we need to be clear about our primary vocation as the followers of Jesus. How is God calling us to serve the present age? The Wesleys prepared every Methodist for the privilege of gospel-bearing in a world parish. What does that mean today?

- Second, a deep awareness of God necessarily leads to prophetic action. The Wesleys lived this pattern and devoted their energy to forming mystic-prophets for the world.

  Leaders like this in the life of Christian community are committed to justice for all.

- Third, living the Wesleyan way means living holistically. The conjunctive nature of Wesleyan theology remains one of its greatest gifts. We believe that honoring nonduality in everything may be one of the greatest needs in our world today.

- Fourth, Jesus came preaching the kingdom of God. God's reign and rule was the central theme of his life and ministry. God's great project of love revolves around our living into the peaceable reign of Christ. We partner with God in this work of shalom.

---

5. Wesley, *Works*, 9:30–46. Steve Harper's book *Five Marks of a Methodist* (Nashville: Abingdon Press, 2015) is a contemporary study of Wesley's "Character of a Methodist."

Living in and for the world today as Methodists means embracing our calling to be gospel-bearers, mystic-prophets, bridge-builders, and shalom-seekers. God calls us today into a life of action in a messy world and to a radical commitment to God's mission of love in and for the world. We have a lot to do! Let's get started so we can translate these conversations into actions.

Conversation 9

Gospel-Bearing in a World Parish

Many thoughtful people are taking a good look at our culture(s) and the gospel today. They are asking questions like, How do we view life? What is our way of living and thinking? And most importantly, How do we live out the gospel in our own context? Likewise, many have come to the conclusion that it is not enough to rehash "how church has always been done." In a post-pandemic world, we cannot simply replicate a pre-pandemic church and think this will work. Too much has changed. But we believe the church also suffers from missional amnesia. It has forgotten some time-tested lessons related to living the faith in the world. Enter the Wesleys. They had the very same questions and concerns that many are asking today. Their response to these questions gave birth to Methodism—the embodiment of missional communities of faith for their time. Living the Wesleyan way includes an ancient-future dynamic well worth exploring.

George Hunsberger, one of the founders of the Gospel and Our Culture movement, is a leading voice in these kind of conversations today. Ironically, his comments from a recent interview provide insight into what the Wesleys were up to nearly 300 years ago:

"Okay, humor me. Aren't there at least some good things to begin doing?"

"Well yes. Absolutely. The missional church responds to the Gospel as its charter story. The Cross has to be a part of the image, and suffering, too. That cuts against the grain of a church that thinks our story has to be a success story."

"What does the missional church look like?"

"A missional church is always being formed as a disciple together, not just a collection of disciples. The pastor's number one calling is to be working at forming a community. A missional church considers its gathered and scattered moments a seamless garment. We are as much a community on Tuesday morning as we are on Sunday morning."

"Missional is a hot term. What is the church's mission?"

"A missional church's mission is to do the kind of deeds in the world that God cares about and intends for our destiny, deeds of justice, peace, care for the creation."[6]

Hunsberger just described earliest Methodism. The Wesleys believed that there must be a vital connection between Christians and the context in which they live out their faith. In order to bear witness to the good news of Jesus Christ, they had to rethink the relation between the gospel and their culture in more dynamic ways. They pressed the question, What is the essential calling of the church? We are convinced that these are some of the most important questions in our time. Addressing them might just trigger a renewal of genuine, authentic faith today. We also believe that "gospel-bearing" through a missional community of love in our world parish provides the key to a future filled with hope.

John and Charles Wesley were unquestionably two of the greatest evangelists of their day. The evangelistic practices of the Wesleys and of the Methodist Societies they founded reflect their understanding of God's character. God is a "missional" God. God is always reaching out. God's grace is active and working to save and restore all creation. The Wesleys attempted to reclaim mission as the church's reason for

6. An edited version of the interview, from "Everything You've Wanted to Know about *Missional* (But Didn't Know to Ask): An interview with George Hunsberger," reported in the Presbyterian Renewal publication, *ReNews*, and shared with the authors.

being and evangelism as the heart of that mission in the world.[7]

We have a good friend who teaches evangelism and mission who always refers to evangelism as the "e" word. Most people fear evangelism. This may be due to the way in which evangelism is portrayed in our cultures in North America. It comes across as something aggressive, abrasive, and combative—even imperialistic. After all, one of the terms most closely associated with it is "crusade." For this reason, and many others, we prefer the term "gospel-bearing" for evangelism. In this conversation we want to unpack what we mean by this and invite you to think about it as a missional practice in our world parish.

First, *gospel-bearing begins with God*. We have already said a great deal about God's character, particularly the centrality of love and grace in God's being and action. Two particular aspects of God's action, however, bear directly on the way we live the good news. Both demonstrate the missional character of God. We have seen, for example, how creation was a sheer act of grace, motivated by nothing other than God's loving nature (see Conversation 5). Incarnation—the act by which God entered human history—demonstrates the same missional quality. Mission means to be sent. Through creation God sends God's love into a newly formed cosmos. Through incarnation God sends the Son to be and enact the word of life.

People today come to know this God through people in whom the essence of God radiates out. God sends us from everywhere to everywhere. God sends us as bearers of God's good news about the love of Christ for all. If this is our calling, what is there to fear? Nothing could be more exciting or exhilarating! What a job? This is our primary vocation, to be gospel and to enact the good news of God's love.

Second, *gospel-bearing is a missional practice of the church*. The Wesleys rediscovered a missional ecclesiology. For them church equals mission. It is not as though the church has a mission; the church is mission. They sought to reclaim participation in God's mission as the primary reason

7. See the excellent discussion of *Evangelism as the Heart of Mission* by Dana L. Robert (New York: General Board of Global Ministries, 1997). See also S T Kimbrough, Jr., ed., *Evangelization, the Heart of Mission: A Wesleyan Imperative* (New York: General Board of Global Ministries, 1995).

for being of the church. They believed that the church was not called to live for itself; rather, it was called to give itself for the life of the world. The church in their time had exchanged this missional calling for maintenance. It had become distant from and irrelevant to the world it was called to serve. The Wesleys helped it reclaim its true identity as God's agent of shalom in the world. Two principles undergirded this vision. First, the community of faith makes disciples who bear witness to the gospel. Second, the church functions itself as evangelist.

The Wesleys firmly believed that God raised up the people called Methodists particularly for the task of resuscitating a missional, evangel-bearing church. The early Methodists viewed themselves as disciples ("learners") of Jesus, not just members of a church. They gathered together in a pilgrim community in order to learn how to love. Then God sent them out ("apostles") to serve the present age by sharing that love with others. They embraced this vocation, not because of what they had done, but because they knew themselves to be God's own people. They were formed by and for God's purpose and grace. Their primary task was to "offer Christ" to everyone everywhere. This gospel-bearing involves both words and deeds, both proclamation and action. It connects the gospel to the world parish.

Third, *gospel-bearing is an all-inclusive practice*. The understanding that God commissioned all believers to be evangelists resonated with this missional vision. The Wesleys encouraged and empowered all their followers to become effective gospel-bearers in the normal round of their ordinary lives. They simply offered the love of Christ to all wherever they were. A vast network of itinerant preacher-evangelists, including women, furthered this mission. It included men women, and children who were black, indigenous, and people of color. John and Charles Wesley excluded none. With them, we believe that all means all. A missional church true to the Wesleys today will be all-inclusive, leaving no one outside the call to bear witness to the gospel in word and deed. All are called to use the gifts God has given them on every level of the community of faith, but following the example of Jesus.

John Wesley offered the following suggestion, therefore, in his *Advice to the People called Methodists*:

> Above all, stand fast in obedient faith, faith in the God of pardoning mercy, in the God and Father of our Lord Jesus Christ, who hath loved you, and given himself for you. Ascribe to him all the good you find in yourself, all your peace, and joy, and love, all your power to do and suffer his will, through the Spirit of the living God. . . . Abhor every approach, in any kind or degree, to the spirit of persecution. If you cannot reason or persuade a man into the truth, never attempt to force him into it. If love will not compel him to come in, leave him to God.[8]

Fourth, *gospel-bearing consists of a network of missional practices.* Five practices stand out in this regard: faithful preaching, inspirational singing, accountable discipleship, authentic worship, and incarnational service.[9] All of these acts of love work together within the context of a missional community. The whole community, in other words, becomes a catalyst of love through these means, all integrated and in sync with God's loving purposes.

(1) *Faithful preaching*. The Wesleys most certainly defined evangelism in terms of verbal proclamation. Eyewitness accounts of John Wesley's own preaching stress the word "now" time and time again. Wesley's persistent theme was simply, "*Now* is the day of salvation" (2 Cor 6:2). In the *Conference Minutes of 1744*, he asked the question, "What is the best general method in preaching?" His fourfold response was simple and clear: "(1) To invite, (2) To convince, (3) To offer Christ. And, lastly, to build up. And to do this (in some measure) in every sermon."[10] The central message was that of universal love to all made known to us in Jesus Christ. Gospel-bearing in the Wesleyan spirit is nothing less than wooing God's children back into God's loving embrace.

The Wesleys launched the Methodist movement, not at the time

8. Wesley, *Works* (Jackson), 8:360.

9. In his Denman Lectures of 1971, *Evangelism in the Wesleyan Spirit* (Nashville: Tidings, 1971), Albert Outler identified three great components of evangelism in the Wesleyan spirit, namely, heralding, martyrdom, and servanthood.

10. Wesley, *Works*, 10:139.

of their "conversions" in 1738, so much as with their "field preaching" in 1739. Instead of waiting for the people to come to them, they took the message of God's unconditional love to the people where they were. The importance of this action cannot be overestimated. The primary content of their preaching is aptly summarized in the so-called "four alls": all need to be saved; all can be saved; all can know they are saved; all can be saved to the uttermost. But their preaching addressed the social evils of their day with equal force. Personal salvation and participation in God's inbreaking reign characterized their evangelistic preaching.

(2) *Accountable discipleship*. The Wesleys believed that gospel-bearing was much more than simply preaching the gospel. Bearing witness to God's love, in fact, took place more fully in the intimacy of small groups than anywhere else. John Wesley emphasized this principle in a journal entry of August 25, 1763: "I was more convinced than ever that the preaching like an apostle, without joining together those that are awakened and training them up in the ways of God, is only begetting children for the murderer."[11] The classes and bands of early Methodism (as we will see more fully in Conversation 11) functioned as potent cells for the promotion of inward and outward holiness. In these small groups dedicated people learned to plumb the depths of God's love for them all and to live that love out in their daily lives.

On the basis of his detailed study of the early Methodist Societies, Tom Albin has argued that most of the early Methodist people were converted, not in response to preaching, but as a consequence of personal relationships with other Christians in the intimacy of small groups.[12] This context proved the most fertile ground for the sharing and nurture of faith. In small groups, faith was born and those awakened were encouraged to grow in grace so as to be channels of love for others. They came to understand their true vocation, and that of the

---

11. John Wesley, *The Works of John Wesley, Volume 21, Journal and Diaries IV (1755–1765)*, ed. W. Reginald Ward and Richard P. Heitzenrater (Nashville: Abingdon Press, 1992), 424.

12. Tom Albin, "Finding God in Small Groups," *Christianity Today* 47, 8 (August 2003): 42–44.

church as the whole people of God, as a summons to enter a particular, revolutionary path of self-sacrificing love for the world. This is how they lived the Wesleyan way.

(3) *Inspirational singing*. The Methodist movement was born in song. Early Methodists found their true identity as the children of God through singing. Singing communicates the faith in a way that sinks deep into the soul. It involves the whole person. Singing pulls head, heart, and hands together as nothing else can do. It is a spiritual exercise. John Wesley describes the primary Methodist hymnal of 1780 as "A Little Body of Experimental and Practical Divinity."[13] The lyrical theology of Charles Wesley both transformed and formed the singer. With regards to the missional practice of gospel-bearing, four primary themes pervade his hymns: the nature of God's unconditional love, the all-sufficiency of God's grace, the all-embracing nature of inclusive community, and the missional vision of God's people.[14]

One of the most popular of Wesley's hymns, "O for a thousand tongues to sing," reflects the missional thrust of this vision. It celebrates the personal experience of salvation. But it also articulates a conception of mission bound to disciples of Jesus committed to spreading the good news of God's love throughout the world.

> My gracious Master, and my God,
> Assist me to proclaim,
> To spread through all the earth abroad
> The honours of thy name.[15]

---

13. John Wesley suggests this in his preface to the *1780 Collection of Hymns for the use of the People Called Methodists*; see Wesley, *Works*, 7:1–22.

14. See Chilcote, *A Faith That Sings*, 116–18; cf. Tore Meistad, "The Missiology of Charles Wesley and Its Links to the Eastern Church," in *Orthodox and Wesleyan Spirituality*, ed. S T Kimbrough Jr. (Crestwood, NY: St. Vladimir's Seminary Press, 2002), 205–31. Meistad concludes that Charles grounded his vision of missional evangelism on the creating, atoning, life-giving Triune God, universal redemption and the person in corporate perspective, salvation conceived as the new creation, love as the manifestation of God's presence, and the messianic kingdom symbolized in the year of Jubilee.

15. Wesley, *Works*, 7:80.

Other hymns, such as "Blow Ye the Trumpet, Blow," pull together Wesley's missional motifs, describing the evangelistic mission of the messianic people in terms of economic justice and human liberation. It is not too much to claim that the early Methodist people sang and discovered their essential identity as gospel-bearers and experienced the inclusivity of the community of faith through the very act of singing together.

(4) *Authentic worship*. It is interesting that John Wesley's original definition of the Methodists revolved around worship. In his *General Rules* he observed:

> A Society is no other than "a company of men [and women] 'having the form, and seeking the power of godliness', united in order to pray together, to receive the word of exhortation, and to watch over one another in love, that they may help each other to work out their salvation."[16]

Authentic worship helps us look upward and inward as a community. A profoundly relational and transformational experience, it reveals the fullness of the gospel and calls for response. The central purpose of worship, as Wesley would have argued, is to present the whole gospel to the whole person. Gospel-bearing, therefore, defines both its content and its character.

The Wesleyan revival was an evangelical reawakening, but it was also a sacramental or Eucharistic revival. The Wesleys believed that their sacramental practice—their frequent celebration of the Lord's Supper—was in every way as evangelistic as their preaching, singing, or interaction with one another in the context of small groups. There was a certain sense in which Holy Communion brought all these practices together in one great sign-act of love.

The sacrament enacts a holistic gospel. It memorializes the passion of Christ, celebrates his living presence as a sign and means of grace, and anticipates the heavenly banquet to come in which God unites

16. John Wesley, *The Works of John Wesley, Volume 9, The Methodist Societies, History, Nature, and Design*, ed. Rupert E. Davies (Nashville: Abingdon Press, 1989), 69.

all God's children in one great feast of love.[17] All these dimensions of the meal communicate the expansive nature of God's good news. The meal offers all this effectively and fully to all who gather around the table. In this sign-act of love, the past, present, and future—faith, hope, and love—are compressed, as it were, into a timeless, communal act of praise.

This "Holy Mystery," as it is also called, creates a particular community with a peculiar calling. Two particular aspects of this creative capacity of the meal shape our gospel-bearing in and for the world. First, the Lord's Supper unites God's people with Christ in a community of joy. It's not too much to say that the sacrament forms the church—the one, holy, apostolic community of God's grace (see 1 Cor 10:17). This meal re-members us. It puts us back together, and the keynote of our fellowship is joy. Wesley sings this so well:

> Our hearts we open wide
> To make the Savior room:
> And lo! The Lamb, the crucified,
> The sinner's friend is come!
> His presence makes the feast,
> And now our bosoms feel
> The glory not to be expressed,
> The joy unspeakable.[18]

Second, this holy meal forms us into a missional community to partner with God in the redemption of the world. In some parts of Africa, the community gathered around the table receives the elements of Communion at the doorway as they depart. They are told, "This is food for your journey. May it strengthen you for all that lies ahead. Share what you received here freely with others." Sometimes they are even given extra food to share with their neighbors. The gospel-bearer,

17. See Wesley, *Hymns on the Lord's Supper*, in which the hymns are divided into sections that reflect these concerns around the themes of the sacrament as a memorial, a means of grace, and a foretaste of the heavenly banquet.

18. Wesley, *Hymns on the Lord's Supper*, 69.

you see, has particular concern for those who are absent from Christ's table—those who feel unworthy, the poor, the unconverted, victims of prejudice, and others who are oppressed or neglected in any way.

(5) *Incarnational service*.[19] Outflow-oriented service also defines gospel-bearing in the Wesleyan way. Inward holiness reflects a habituated interior love (love of God). Loving service to others in imitation of Christ reveals and enlarges an outward holiness (love of others). Faithful witness to God's love requires both. Familiar words from the pen of Charles Wesley strike this diaconal chord:

> A charge to keep I have,
> A God to glorify,
> A never-dying soul to save,
> And fit it for the sky;
> To serve the present age,
> My calling to fulfil;
> O may it all my powers engage
> To do my Master's will.[20]

What does this look like specifically? Well, to be a Wesleyan gospel-bearer means, first and foremost, to do evangelism in the way of Jesus. His self-giving love is the goal, purpose, and style for living the Wesleyan way. Second, the servant offers to others what he or she has freely received from God. Christlike, missional evangelism offers God's grace to all in both word and deed. Third, to have the mind of Christ—to be a gospel-bearer—entails the care of the poor and the dispossessed. Living the Wesleyan way means opening your heart to God's healing love. It means longing to radiate the whole image of God in your life *and therefore* hearing the cry of those who suffer in any way. The gospel-bearer wills, with God, that all should truly live!

This Wesleyan vision of mission, properly understood, is *a life*, not just an act. Living into this vision unites piety and mercy, worship and compassion, prayer and justice. It involves a humble walk with

---

19. We will explore this theme more fully in the final Conversation on living into the peaceable reign of Christ.

20. Wesley, *Scripture Hymns*, 1:58.

the Lord that is lived out daily in kindness and justice. Living into God's upward call means that you proclaim and embody the whole gospel for the whole person throughout the whole world through this holistic network of missional practices. It is the normal work of the whole church all the time.

In his hymn, "For a Preacher of the Gospel," Charles Wesley reminds us of this transforming call of God upon our lives to be gospel-bearers in a world parish:

I would the precious time redeem
And longer live for this alone,
To spend and to be spent for them
Who have not yet my Saviour known:
Fully on these my mission prove,
And only breathe to breathe thy love.[21]

21. Wesley, *Hymns and Sacred Poems* (1749), 1:300.

Reflection Questions

Conversation 9 (Gospel-Bearing)

1. What part of this Conversation spoke most to you? Why is it important for you to hear this right now?

2. How does thinking about "evangelism" as everyday "gospel-bearing" change your attitude about it?

3. To which of the various missional practices associated with gospel-bearing are you most naturally drawn?

Conversation 10

Forming Mystic-Prophets for the World

As children of the 1960s, both of us could hardly resist reading what is now a classic in the Catholic spiritual tradition—*On Becoming a Musical, Mystical Bear*—when it first hit the bookstores in the early 1970s. It had us at the title. It's author, Matthew Fox, continues to be one of the most challenging spiritual teachers of our time. We catch several of his statements here about an event related to awakening modern mystics and prophets.[1]

"History is filled with bold activists, brave rebels, and radical agents for change. . . . Their lives and lifework were dedicated to speaking truth, carrying the message of love, and serving the greater good.

"And, your own chosen path is actually a response to this same calling to serve the planet and future generations. To become a modern mystic and prophet—a lover and warrior—a 'disruptor' and catalyst for profound change.

"The wisdom and power of the great mystics and prophets is not just reserved for a select few, or only for ordained messengers. These qualities live within *you,* and they can empower you on your own journey.

"With a world rife with division, now is a time for equipping,

1. "Awaken Modern Mystics and Prophets," The Shift Network; https://theshiftnetwork.com/ModernMysticsProphets; accessed January 22, 2023.

empowering, and building capacity for today's modern mystics and prophets."

John and Charles Wesley were mystic-prophets of this order. In fact, this is a rather perfect description of who they were and what they did. This also characterized the ambiance of their renewal in the life of the church. We have studied many different Christian renewal movements. They all share a number of characteristics in common like the rediscovery of the Bible, living faith, authentic worship, accountable discipleship, and missional vocation.[2] In this conversation we want to highlight just one of these—Christian spirituality as the synthesis of action and contemplation. Like Matthew Fox today, the Wesleys were lovers who said Yes to life (mystics) and warriors who said No to lies and injustice in its many forms in their own time (prophets). We need these kinds of Christians today more than ever. We are convinced that living the Wesleyan way is advanced through mystic-prophets who live deeply in God, and then live broadly in the world to do good.[3] This is one way by which we live in and for the world.

One of the great misconceptions in religion is that becoming contemplative imprisons us in interiority. To be sure, there are some kinds of contemplation that do this. The Wesleys discerned this aberration in writers and movements given over to Quietism.[4] In fact, John Wesley went so far as to say that in response to this he was done with the mystics. But a closer look reveals that he was saying "good-bye" to a deformative mysticism akin to the kind James eschewed when he wrote that faith without works or actions is dead (James 2:26). Our study of the Wesleys, however, demonstrates that both brothers continued to be influenced by contemplatives who practiced works of mercy—those they would describe as practical mystics, like Thomas à Kempis.

---

2. See Paul W. Chilcote, *The Wesleyan Tradition: A Paradigm for Renewal* (Nashville: Abingdon Press, 2002).

3. Matthew Fox is well known today for his use of the term "mystic-prophet" in his book *On Becoming a Musical, Mystical Bear* (Mahwah: Paulist Press, 1972). Fox revised and republished this book under the title *Prayer, a Radical Response to Life* (New York: Tarcher, 2001).

4. See Robert Tuttle, *Mysticism in the Wesleyan Tradition* (Grand Rapids: Zondervan, 1989).

The Wesleys were drawn into this life to a large extent through the reading of biographies. For example, John Wesley wrote of the influence of Jean-Baptiste de Renty upon him.[5] De Renty, a French nobleman (1611–1649 CE), lived his faith in a general pattern of morning contemplation and afternoon action. This confirmed to John that the spiritual life could be lived as a seamless garment of piety and mercy, Following the example of de Renty and others who lived similarly, he ordered his life in this general pattern. Robert Tuttle describes this lifestyle a "mysticism of service."[6] In people such as de Renty, the Wesleys saw what life looks like in a union of spirituality and social consciousness or benevolence.

The Wesleys held together, in other words, a religion of the heart (interior spirituality) expressed in witness and service in the world (exterior spirituality). To use the categories of Richard Foster's streams of spirituality, they combined a prayer-filled, Spirit-empowered life with a compassionate, world-centered life.[7] They embodied and enacted the essence of a mystic-prophet life. Those who abide deeply with God in the heart cultivate hearts that are like God's—full of love for all and moved to live for their good.[8] This reflects an important paradox about life in Christ that the Wesleys embraced wholeheartedly—the farther inward we go into God the more outward we will go into the world.[9] Immersion into God's love makes us loving. That's why the two great

---

5. John Wesley, *An Extract of the Life of Monsieur de Renty: A Late Nobleman of France* (Bristol: Grabham & Pine, 1760).

6. Tuttle, *Mysticism in the Wesleyan Tradition*, 162.

7. See "The Six Streams: A Balanced Vision, Renovaré Institute": https://renovare.org/about/ideas/the-six-streams; accessed January 22, 2023.

8. Ted A. Campbell, *The Religion of the Heart* (Eugene: Wipf & Stock, 2000) offers an excellent study of the subject. Gregory S. Clapper focuses the idea in the Wesleyan tradition in his books, *As if the Heart Mattered* (Nashville: Upper Room Books, 1997) and *The Renewal of the Heart in the Mission of the Church* (Eugene: Cascade Books, 2010).

9. We find this paradoxical contemplation/action model in spiritual leaders of different religious traditions such as Mohandas Gandhi, Thomas Merton, Dorothy Day, Thich Nhat Hanh, Oscar Romero, John Dear, and Lisa Sharon Harper—to name a few.

commandments—love of God and love of neighbor—go together to create a singular spirituality. Genuine mystics know this and live accordingly.

We note this formative interiority particularly in the Wesleyan emphasis on prayer. Charles Wesley concludes a poetic exposition of the whole armor of God with these memorable words about prayer:

> Pray, without ceasing pray
> (Your Captain gives the word),
> His summons cheerfully obey,
> And call upon the Lord;
> To God your every want
> In instant prayer display;
> Pray always; pray, and never faint;
> Pray, without ceasing pray.[10]

You just want to ask, Is anyone confused? John Wesley once referred to prayer as "the grand means of drawing near to God, and all others [means of grace] are helpful to us only so far as they are mixed with or prepare us for this."[11] The Christian life is relational and experiential first and foremost with respect to God. From the cultivation of prayer (private and public, spontaneous and liturgical) we live as God intends. Here again we see the Wesleys' conviction that living deeply in God propels us into living well in the world.

The mystics contributed to this view of prayer through their understanding of it as a disposition of the heart. John Wesley noted the contributions of de Renty, Gregory Lopez, and Francois Fenelon on his own spiritual development in this regard. In fact, John Wesley's *A Collection of Forms of Prayer for Each Day of the Week* (1733) may have been designed in relation to mystical prayer, where the themes of self-examination, humility, mortification, and resignation are utilized.[12] He also rooted the *Collection* in the two great commandments (Sunday and Monday themes) from which "the fire of love" ignites and spreads.

---

10. Wesley, *Hymns and Sacred Poems* (1749), 1:238.

11. John Wesley, *The Works of John Wesley, Volume 27, Letters III, 1756–1765*, ed. Ted A. Campbell (Nashville: Abingdon, 2015), 190.

12. Tuttle, *Mysticism in the Wesleyan Tradition*, 159.

First, *the mystic heritage has much to offer us today.* Moving all of this into the present, the mystical way is receiving fresh attention in the growing contemplative movement. Matthew Fox has emphasized that prayer is not a withdrawal from one's culture or acquiescence to culture; it is an engagement with culture. "Prayer takes place," he writes, "as a wrestling with the spiritual powers and principalities (where spiritual means deep, living, and real) of one's world, of one's culture."[13] We emphasized this in the previous conversation. Here we show the central role which prayer plays in that engagement. Prayer gives us the eyes to see things realistically and the will to change them transformationally.

Language related to the heart, something dear to the Wesleys, provides fitting imagery in this conversation about mystic-prophets. The lifeblood of God flows into our hearts via the veins (works of piety) and then flows out of our hearts into the world via the arteries (works of mercy). It is easy to see again the Celtic ambiance in this—listening and acting with the sense of liberation that the Spirit effects inwardly and outwardly.[14] In a formative sense, this recognition and response of the mystic-prophet life finds unique expression in the Covenant Renewal Service. The Wesleys invited the Methodists annually to recognize their call to service and to respond positively.

The recognition occurred in the words:

> Christ has many services to be done.
> Some are more easy and honorable,
> others are more difficult and disgraceful.
> Some are suitable to our inclinations and interests,
> others are contrary to both.
> In some we may please Christ and please ourselves.
> But then there are other works where we cannot please Christ
> except by denying ourselves.

---

13. Matthew Fox, *Prayer, A Radical Response to Life*, 6–14. Quote on page 10.

14. J. Philip Newell, *Listening for the Heartbeat of God: A Celtic Spirituality* (Mahwah: Paulist Press, 1997), 1–2.

> Yet the power to do all these things is given to us in Christ,
> who strengthens us.[15]

The historic "covenant prayer" itself articulates the response:

> I am no longer my own, but thine.
> Put me to what thou wilt, rank me with whom thou wilt.
> Put me to doing, put me to suffering.
> Let me be employed by thee or laid aside for thee,
> exalted for thee or brought low for thee.
> Let me be full, let me be empty.
> Let me have all things, let me have nothing.
> I freely and heartily yield all things
> to thy pleasure and disposal.
> And now, O glorious and blessed God,
> Father, Son, and Holy Spirit,
> thou art mine, and I am thine. So be it.
> And the covenant which I have made on earth,
> let it be ratified in heaven. Amen.[16]

The Covenant Renewal Service continues to be a valuable means for shaping the mystic-prophet life. Magrey deVega has studied the service, noting that it helps us "to remember that though we have finite, limited, and mortal lives, we have the capacity in Christ to make an eternal impact for God's kingdom."[17] His words connect our life of prayer with our prophetic calling. First, and importantly, we remember that prophets are ordinary people. Amos was a shepherd. Anna was an old woman. They were prophets, not because they were extraordinary, but because they had a vision of a new creation that generated their efforts to bring it to pass.

---

15. "Covenant Renewal Service," Discipleship Ministries, The United Methodist Church; https://www.umcdiscipleship.org/resources/covenant-renewal-service; accessed January 22, 2023.

16. *United Methodist Hymnal*, 607. Note the associations with St. Paul's exhortation to become living sacrifices (Rom 12:1).

17. Magrey R. deVega, *One Faithful Promise: The Wesleyan Covenant for Renewal* (Nashville: Abingdon Press, 2016), 7.

Second, *mystic awareness leads to prophetic action.* Prophets, far from being conveyors of gloom-and-doom, are bearers of light and hope. We like to call them God's "imagineers," those who see a dying world in the context of resurrection.[18] Walter Brueggemann calls this the prophetic imagination.[19] Gordon Wakefield has shown how the Wesleys incarnated the spirit and ministries of the prophets, referring to the Wesleyan movement as a radical spirituality.[20] Ilia Delio has written about this broad-spectrum contemplation:

> Contemplative vision is the heart of the Christian life by which we are brought into a new reality, connected through the heart to the whole of life, attuned to the deeper intelligence of nature, and called forth irresistibly by the Spirit to creatively express our gifts in the evolution of self and world.[21]

The ministry of the prophet follows the pattern of calling out societal sin, calling for repentance, and calling forth hope.[22] This model begins with naming and wrestling with the "principalities and powers" (individually and collective) of the fallen world. It is a confrontation that challenges us to envision a new way of life made possible by God's grace. With that vision, we live with the hope that we are on the way to a time when the kingdoms of this world will become the kingdom of God and of Christ (Rev 11:15). We see this pattern in the ministries of the Wesleys and in the early Methodist movement.

No injustice in the Wesleys' day brought out this prophetic spirit in John more than the British slave trade and the practice of slavery itself.

---

18. Steve Harper, "At the Gate: Imagineers," *Oboedire* blogpost, January 2, 2023; https://oboedire.wordpress.com/2023/01/02/at-the-gate-imagineers/; accessed January 22, 2023.

19. Walter Brueggemann, *The Prophetic Imagination,* rev. ed. (Minneapolis: Fortress Press, 2001).

20. Gordon S. Wakefield, *Methodist Spirituality* (London: Epworth Press, 1999), 81–82.

21. Delio, *The Hours of the Universe,* 167

22. Walter Brueggemann, *Reality, Grief, Hope: Three Urgent Prophetic Tasks* (Grand Rapids: Eerdmans, 2014).

He did not mince his words. His questions cut deep. They had to when he was dealing with those who marketed in human beings:

> May I speak plainly to you? I must. Love constrains me; love to you, as well as to those you are concerned with. Is there a God? You know there is. . . . Are you a human being? Then you should have a human heart. But have you indeed? What is your heart made of? Is there no such principle as compassion there? Do you never feel another's pain? Have you no sympathy, no sense of human woe, no pity for the miserable? When you saw the flowing eyes, the heaving breasts, or the bleeding sides and tortured limbs of your fellow creatures, were you a stone, or a brute?[23]

In a hymn based on Isaiah's iconic vision (11:6-7), Charles views the world realistically, but promotes God's transformational grace as the vehicle of change:

Prince of universal peace,
Destroy the enmity,
Bid our jars and discords cease,
Unite us all in thee.
Cruel as wild beasts we are,
'Till vanquished by thy mercy's power,
We, like wolves, each other tear,
And their own flesh devour.

But if thou pronounce the word
That forms our souls again,
Love and harmony restored
Throughout the earth shall reign;
When thy wondrous love they feel,
The human savages are tame,
Ravenous wolves, and leopards dwell
And stable with the lamb.[24]

23. John Wesley, "Thoughts upon Slavery," in *Works* (Jackson), 11:76–77.
24. Wesley, *Scripture Hymns*, 1:316.

Third, *justice characterizes the life of the mystic-prophet.* The efforts required to effect fairness, equity, and inclusion in the world must be both deep and wide. This demands both praying and prophesying for the common good. We remember our call to "to do justice and to love kindness and to walk humbly with your God" (Micah 6:8). In that vision we pray in the spirit of Amos to "let justice roll down like waters, and righteousness like an ever-flowing stream" (Amos 5:24). And then, we live like Jesus, who "traveled around doing good" (Acts 10:38).

The life of a mystic-prophet is vocational; it is exercised in the daily round of ordinary activities where we find God as Mother Teresa affirmed with such power, in the distressing disguise of the poor. Methodists seem to have been born for this, or perhaps it was the other way around. Could it be that the life into which the Wesleys invited them shaped them into the kind of people who found their true vocation in the mystic-prophet life? Regardless, the movement was made up largely of laity who lived for Christ within the context of their vocations. You cannot impose or add a mystic-prophet identity to someone's life. Reading the world realistically and engaging in transformative justice is a natural expression that flows from hearts filled with God and turned towards the world. The "many services" we perform in and for the world both express and shape the child of God we are and are becoming.

As we embrace the mystic-prophet life—as we integrate it into our lives as we are and where we are—we discern signs that we are living faithfully in our day in the world in Jesus' name. Matthew Fox provides four indications with regard to living this life: personal rerooting and becoming radical lovers, humble reluctance to claim our prophetic role so that God may remain central, creativity that generates new things and which supports already-existing creativity, and doing all this in community.[25]

Fourth, *mystic-prophets will inevitably encounter persecution.* We dare not omit this final aspect of the mystic-prophet life. Mystic-prophets do not seek opposition or wear it as a badge of honor. But they know that seeing and living differently will receive pushback from those who

25. Fox, *Prayer, a Radical Response to Life*, 109–15.

have made the status quo a sacred cow and have benefitted by doing so. The Hebrew prophets experienced persecution, as did Jesus, the early Christians, and so many since. The Wesleys did too, and so will we if we decide to embrace the mystic-prophet life. Sadly, the story of history reminds us that this persecution comes sometimes from fellow Christians and from inside the church.

Soren Kierkegaard, a nineteenth-century mystic-prophet of the Danish state church, maintained that the authentic Christian life must be lived against the crowd, and even more painfully, against the church. He grieved for those Christians whose lives seemed to bear no resemblance to the life of Jesus. In the previous century, the Wesleys were opposed by professing Christians who had sold their souls to values that were not Christlike. They succumbed to the temptations of materialism, hedonism, and power. Sometimes it seems as though little changes.

We conclude this conversation with this note of realism because we live the mystic-prophet life by going through trials, not by going around them. Mystic-prophets are hopeful realists, never ignoring the things which destroy life, but refusing to believe they will prevail. Mystic-prophets believe in the final triumph of righteousness, and act in congruence with it. The mystic-prophet who lives the Wesleyan way confronts the personal malaise, the ecclesial amnesia, and the social injustice with the knowledge that love and justice will triumph in the end.

Perhaps this all boils down to a simple phrase our longtime friend and colleague, Jerry Mercer, used to describe the essence of Wesleyan spirituality: "living deeply our new life in Christ."[26] We have no doubt that the Wesleys would commend it. David Hinton captures the essence and energy of the mystic-prophet life in a slightly different way that captures the paradox of the mystic and the prophet: "cultivation of wholeness for self is, miraculously, also cultivation of wholeness for the planet."[27] Moving upward in Wesleyan formation is living as a mystic-prophet in and for the world.

---

26. Jerry L. Mercer, *Living Deeply Our New Life in Christ* (Nashville: Discipleship Resources, 1999).

27. David Hinton, *Wild Mind, Wild Earth* (Boston: Shambhala, 2022), 47.

Reflection Questions

Conversation 10 (Mystic-Prophets)

1. What part of this Conversation spoke most to you? Why is it important for you to hear this right now?

2. When you look at your life through the lens of a mystic, what do you see?

3. When you look at your life through the lens of a prophet, what do you see?

Conversation 11

Honoring Nonduality in Everything

We had the great privilege of sharing the same mentors. They not only shaped us as scholars of the Wesleyan tradition but lived authentically as Christians before us. They were always seeking to find ways to bring different people together. They were uniters, and we pray that some of their spirit rubbed off on us. They were ecumenists within Christianity, and interfaith advocates beyond it. They were bridge builders. They did all of this out of the Wesleyan conviction that living faith is the turning of intangible affirmations into concrete actions, words into deeds. They understood that the word salvation means wholeness, and they devoted their lives to advancing the common good.

In one conversation with Frank Baker, Paul remembers asking him about how he deals with tensions in the church. This was long before the kind of animosity we experience today had erupted. He was also interested in how Dr. Baker navigated debate with his colleagues when differences of opinion became sharp. So Paul simply asked him, "How do you deal with this kind of stuff?"

His reply was terse and straight to the point. "Never focus your attention on winning. Always attempt to be as irenic as you can be." He had a large view of things. He always extended a large embrace.

So did Nellie Baker, his wife. Thursday evenings we would often go to the gym on East Campus at Duke to play badminton. The vast majority of people there were Asian. Paul remembers Nellie saying,

"Many of these students have no contact with anyone outside their circle of Asian friends. I think many of them are lonely. We knew that they loved badminton, and so do we. So Frank and I started this club to give them a place to meet others, relax, and enjoy a good time with us."

It was Nellie, and not Frank, who said to Paul one day: "You know, there would have been no Methodism without both brothers, John and Charles. They belong together in the story of our church."

Frank and Nellie Baker built bridges. They held things together. They refused to think in terms of "either/or." And this was true for them in every aspect of life (except Duke basketball perhaps).

We are the heirs of their witness, and this book is an homage to them. Beyond a doubt, the Wesleys felt and lived the same way. The Methodist movement, in and of itself, and in collaboration with other groups, engaged in a host of ministries that united the spiritual and the physical, the visible and invisible, in restorative actions. Living the Wesleyan way means honoring nonduality in everything.

This means living incarnationally. The Word became flesh in Jesus, and it is meant to become so in us as well. The Incarnation represents a kind of cosmic "bridge building" and the removal of dividing walls (Eph 2:14). John Wesley called this ministry of Christ "the very bond and center of union," that created "one mystical body."[1] The Wesleys lived out this vision, and from the Incarnation of Christ and their embodiment of it (Christlikeness) in their day, we receive our marching orders for today. In fact, we are not hesitant to say that honoring nonduality in everything is the most important element in Wesleyan formation.

Incarnational living unites word and flesh, belief and practice. As we showed in Conversation 5, the Wesleys saw this in the first creation and understood that it was the trajectory we are on as we move into the new creation. The person of Jesus and his message of the kingdom of God are the confirmations of unitive thinking and living.[2] Simply put, the gospel does not separate spirit and matter.

In Wesleyan theology, this union includes an eschatological component. When the risen Christ judges the nations in Matthew 25,

1. Wesley, *New Testament Notes*, comments on Eph 2:14-15.

2. E. Stanley Jones, *The Unshakable Kingdom and the Unchanging Person* (Nashville: Abingdon Press, 1972), the next-to-the-last book Jones wrote, a gathering up of the notes of his Christology into a symphony.

it is in relation to tangibles: feeding the hungry, giving water to the thirsty, welcoming the stranger, clothing the naked, caring for the sick, and visiting prisoners. The Methodist movement (beginning with the Holy Club at Oxford) manifested all these practices through a variety of ministries. John Wesley rooted incarnational living in the nature of God, whom he referred to as "the Father of all light, material or spiritual." He believed that living in the light and being light bearers in the world proved our holiness as "the imitators of God."[3]

Charles Wesley sang about a woman he considered to be holy in this way. In his lyrical portrait of Mary Naylor—one of the Methodist leaders in Bristol—he provides a real life illustration of this point. He excludes none from this vision and goal:

> The golden rule she has pursued,
> And did to others as she would
> Others should do to her;
> Justice composed her upright soul,
> Justice did all her thoughts control,
> And formed her character.
>
> A nursing mother to the poor,
> For them she husbanded her store,
> Her life, her all, bestowed;
> For them she labored day and night,
> In doing good her whole delight,
> In copying after God.[4]

Evidence of the works of mercy further confirm that God's upward call means to follow Jesus in doing good to others in material ways. Charles demonstrated the inseparability of the spiritual and physical in this hymn on Acts 20:35:

> Work for the weak, and sick, and poor,
> Clothing and food for them procure,
> And mindful of God's word,

3. Wesley, *New Testament Notes*, comments on James 2:17 and 1 John 1:7.

4. Charles Wesley, *Funeral Hymns* (Bristol: Farley, 1759), 53.

Enjoy the blessedness to give,
Lay out your substance to relieve
The members of your Lord.

Your labor which proceeds from love,
Jesus shall graciously approve,
With full felicity,
With brightest crowns your loan repay,
And tell you in that joyful day,
"Ye did it unto Me."[5]

We often think of eschatology in very abstract and theoretical ways. But for the Wesleys, the reign of God breaks into our world through the actions of ordinary people. There is nothing abstract about it; northing could be more concrete. Theologically, we call this realized eschatology—the reign of God manifest through tangible expressions. The healing ministry of Jesus was a paramount sign that the kingdom of heaven was near. The early Christian community continued Jesus' healing ministry and broadened it to include the stewardship of resources so that none were left in need (Acts 2:45 and 4:34).

Wherever the Gospel has gone, redemption and lift have occurred, advancing the common good, with particular care for those whom Jesus called "the least of these"—those who were marginalized, overlooked, and demeaned by fallen-world imperialism. Looking at the Wesleyan tradition, Colin Morris wrote, "There is a real sense in which John Wesley stressed realized eschatology more than any other western theologian."[6] The Wesleyan emphasis on both Incarnation and eschatology teaches us several important lessons about moving upward in Wesleyan formation.

First, *nondual thinking provides a robust vision of life*. We feel fortunate to be living in a time when nondual thinking is reviving. The discoveries of science have fueled these developments. They reveal the oneness of all things from the smallest particle to the farthest star.[7] A

5. Charles Wesley, MS Acts, 419.

6. Morris, *John Wesley's Theology Today*, 194.

7. We point to the Center for Christogenesis and the Nautilus Institute as two examples of organizations that are advancing the renaissance of nonduality.

leader in the Nautilus Institute explains the expanding vision of science in these words:

> People have lost their capacity for experiencing the wonder of not being able to understand something, of not being able to explain things that are mysterious. For us the experience of wonder leads us to change. It enables us to expand our imagination. It leads us to a space of creativity where we can make life sweeter for us now and in the future.[8]

We are moved by these words of science because they so closely parallel what we are saying. They confirm in scientific language what Jesus taught in the first Beatitude—that humility is the first step into the blessed life, the step which stimulates creativity and change and improves life for all.

In concert with the sciences, theology increasingly voices the message that we exist in a cosmic oneness where everything belongs.[9] This view emerges from the combination of wisdom and wonder which we have emphasized in the first two movements of this book. This vision arises in every culture through mystic-prophets, as we have shown in the last two conversations. We believe wholeheartedly that the Wesleys would welcome this revival of nondual thinking and celebrate the fact that they have contributed to it in their own way.

Perhaps their greatest contribution comes from the conjunctive method they used across the spectrum of their theological work. The first paper Paul ever wrote on Wesleyan theology he entitled "Both/And."[10] Both of us have made this nondual, synthetic approach a major emphasis in our Wesleyan scholarship. This way of thinking simply permeates John's theological discourse and Charles's lyrical theology. They exhibit an organic understanding of theology, which can be

8. Nautilus Institute, "The Most Beautiful Science of the Year" (December 28, 2022).

9. Richard Rohr, *Everything Belongs*, Revised and Expanded Edition (New York: Crossroad, 2003) is a good introduction to nondual thinking and living.

10. Chilcote, *Recapturing the Wesleys' Vision*, 11.

described in separate parts, but only gives life when kept together as a whole, with its broadest expression in the union of heaven and earth.

Ecotheology today exhibits this nondual thinking. Howard Snyder brings the Wesleyan tradition into an engaging conversation with regards to the integration of ecology and theology. This has become one of his greatest passions. He feels so strongly about this that he asserts creation care should be added to the Wesleyan quadrilateral, turning it into a pentalateral.[11] His conviction for doing this is simple: if the earth dies, nothing else matters. And while the Wesleys cannot be called environmentalists in the contemporary sense of the term, Snyder does believe their theology sets a trajectory for thinking and living environmentally.[12]

Second, ***the Wesleyan synthesis of faith and form illustrates nondual thinking.*** While more could be said about Wesleyan theology as an expression of nondual thinking and living, we believe that the Wesleyan synthesis of faith and form has great contemporary significance. Our particular interest in this regard revolves around the understanding that the structures of the Methodist movement were containers to hold and dispense their theology of "faith working by love." When Steve co-authored a book with Robert Wilson on this topic, they showed how Methodist theology and polity are a seamless garment.[13] Drawing on the wisdom of organizational theory (that every system manufactures what it is designed to produce), they sought to show that the Wesleys conscientiously developed a sociology of religion as a wineskin to contain and pour out the wine of their theology. There was a "method" in Methodism that created a formative environment in which to nurture holiness of heart and life.

The Methodist Societies were the vehicles for the operation of

---

11. Howard Snyder, "Holistic Mission and the Wesleyan Pentalateral" (an unpublished paper he delivered in 2006).

12. Howard Snyder, "Wesley the Environmentalist?" (Catalyst Resources, published online on February 1, 2009).

13. Robert L. Wilson and Steve Harper, *Faith and Form: A Unity of Theology and Polity in the United Methodist Tradition* (Grand Rapids: Zondervan, 1988).

prevenient grace, where people brought their first desire to please God to a community that welcomed them and offered basic instruction in how to kindle the flame of that desire. The classes afforded a space for seekers to experience convincing and justifying grace. In these small groups the witness of faithful Christians facilitated conversion among those who yearned to know God. Here they experienced the exhilaration of pardon and new birth in their lives. Interestingly, it was not under the preaching of the Wesleys or their itinerant preachers that most early Methodists experienced conversion. Conversion happened in the intimacy of these small groups.

The bands provided "life together" for sanctifying grace to mature inwardly and outwardly. The penitent bands gave strugglers a place to recover and resume their faith journey. And the select societies were groups where those making particular progress in their faith could receive even more personal encouragement. The annual conference was where the leaders met to discern what to teach, how to teach, and what to do—making Minutes which they then used to communicate and resource their decisions.[14]

Most structures function to constrain and control. Not these Wesleyan institutions. One of the most amazing qualities of the small groups, in particular, was their capacity to empower and liberate. Most often the groups included both women and men (with leaders of both genders), but there were times when formation occurred best when men met with men, and women met with women. Resisting a one-size-fits-all pattern, the Methodist movement expressed a contextualized synthesis of spirit and substance. It was an amazing method. This was all part of John Wesley's organizational genius.

There are signs that the Wesleys designed Methodism to be an expression of Third Orders where lay-led renewal of church and the reformation of society through ministries to the marginalized was the driving force of its mission. Like Third Orders within the Roman Catholic tradition, Methodism had a Minister General (John Wesley), a Constitution ("The Character of a Methodist"), a Rule ("The General

14. John Wesley, *The Works of John Wesley, Volume 10, The Methodist Societies.*

Rules of the United Societies"), a meeting of the Order (Annual Conference), and a means for renewing the fellowship (Covenant Renewal Service).

All of this, as is the case in Third Orders as well, remained within the larger structure of the church, not separate from it. Methodism was meant to be an *ecclesiola in ecclesia* (a little church in the big church), not a movement separate from the Church. John Wesley made this point repeatedly, never apologizing for calling himself a Church of England man. He always viewed Methodism as a movement of renewal that represented the Christian faith in that ecclesiastical structure.[15] It was not until John Wesley saw that the future of Methodism lay outside any particular denomination that he began to take actions to perpetuate Methodism after his death. He saw the handwriting on the wall, but as long as he lived, Methodism was not a denomination.

Third, *the Wesleyan synthesis of spiritual and physical offers an important corrective to distortions of Christian living today.* We are sick unto death because of our many divisions. Partisanship with its never-ending supremacies and competitions is doing great harm to the human family, to the planet, and to the Body of Christ. As those in the Wesleyan tradition we must remember that "doing no harm" is our first General Rule. As we have shown, the will and the means to do this emerges from the nondual vision expressed in Paul's words, "you are all one in Christ Jesus" (Gal 3:28). We have tried to show throughout how, for the Wesleys, all means all. Reflecting their nondual way of thinking, the Wesleys add a second General Rule to this admonition to do no harm. Do all the good you can. They were convinced that living holistically in the Spirit generates compassion and the desire to meet the physical needs of people and resist the things that deprive them of life.

Fourth, *living in ways that honor nonduality requires courage.* We cannot end this conversation without noting that a commitment to nonduality will be resisted by "the principalities and powers" who hold

15. Frank Baker, *John Wesley and the Church of England* (Nashville: Abingdon Press, 1970) is the most extensive study of the relationship between the Church of England and John Wesley's Methodism.

power, exercise control, and make money off of fragmentation. We saw this in the last conversation about mystic-prophets, showing how a life that moves from contemplation to action will be controversial. When we adopt nonduality, we must do so courageously. Parker Palmer has written about this, calling such courage "standing in the tragic gap" between vision and reality.[16] And he founded what came to be called the Center for Courage Renewal in 1997, precisely because he saw a lack of courage inhibiting the advance of good in the world.

The Wesleys were no strangers to pushback. They were called on the carpet by bishops, ostracized by colleagues, shouted down and even stoned by mobs. Some Methodists lost property, and occasionally their lives for incarnating a nondual vision aimed at doing good to all (Gal 6:10), which meant calling unjust structures into question. The Methodists advanced, as did the early Christian movement, on the heels of courage, saying as the first apostles did, "we must obey God rather than humans" (Acts 5:29). Proclaiming the gospel in its nondual, inclusive form is always opposed by those who prefer darkness to light. Lighting a candle in such a world takes courage, even so in parts of the church.[17]

Bringing this conversation to a close is difficult. There is so much that we have left unsaid, for there are so many ways dualism is perpetrated today. But returning to the note that nonduality is a way to describe Wesleyan realized eschatology, we conclude by moving into the vision of the new creation (an eternal nonduality comprised of a new heaven and a new earth), a fullness of faith in the fullness of time. St. John described this vision with reference to "a great crowd that no one could number. They were from every nation, tribe, people, and language" (Rev 7:9). In the face of this eventuality, living the Wesleyan way means echoing what St. John said at the end of his revelation: "Amen. Come, Lord Jesus" (Rev 22:20)!

---

16. Parker Palmer, *A Hidden Wholeness*, 180.
17. Christian Nationalism is an anti-gospel that resists the nondual message we have commended here.

Reflection Questions

Conversation 11 (Nonduality)

1. Which part of this Conversation spoke most to you? Why is it important for you to hear this right now?

2. How do you see yourself as a bridge-builder?

3. Which structures have been most beneficial to you in your spiritual formation?

Conversation 12

Living into the Peaceable Reign of Christ

On July 12, 2019, Coretta Scott King posted on Facebook about her husband's dream of the "beloved community." This exchange reveals the lasting influence of Dr. King's vision.

"Do you believe your husband's vision is still viable?"

"To me, the Beloved Community is a realistic vision of an achievable society, one in which problems and conflict exist, but are resolved peacefully and without bitterness."

"How do you describe this vision in your own words?"

"The Beloved Community is a state of heart and mind, a spirit of hope and goodwill that transcends all boundaries and barriers and embraces all creation. At its core, the Beloved Community is an engine of reconciliation."

"So what must we do to realize this vision?"

"This way of living seems a long way from the kind of world we have now, but I do believe it is a goal that can be accomplished through courage and determination, and through education and training, if enough people are willing to make the necessary commitment."[1]

"Beloved community" was the term Martin Luther King, Jr. used

1. See https://www.facebook.com/corettascottking/posts/to-me-the-beloved-community-is-a-realistic-vison-of-an-achievable-society-one-i/689076578230095/; accessed January 10, 2023.

for the "kingdom of God."[2] Walter Brueggemann identifies God's rule with the singular Hebrew term—"shalom"—which he defines as a vision of "a caring, sharing, rejoicing community with none to make them afraid."[3] The terms "beloved community" and "shalom" function as shorthand for a profound and dynamic conception of God's rule. Everything in the universe moves towards this goal.

Charles Wesley describes the kingdom of God as the "quiet and peaceable reign."[4] He describes some of the dimensions of this rule in one of his hymns. He prays for God's kingdom to come. He celebrates its realization in the here and now. He admonishes everyone to live into this alternative reality with hope. The hymn concludes with a prayer to Jesus:

> Come then to thy servants again,
>   Who long thy appearing to know,
> Thy quiet and peaceable reign
>   In mercy establish below:
> All sorrow before thee shall fly,
>   And anger and hatred be o'er,
> And envy and malice shall die,
>   And discord afflict us no more.[5]

Like his brother, John recognized both the present and future dimensions of God's reign. He reflects on this in his note on Matthew 3:2: "The kingdom of heaven and the kingdom of God are but two phrases for the same thing. They mean, not barely a future happy state,

---

2. Kenneth L. Smith and Ira G. Zepp, Jr., *Search for the Beloved Community: The Thinking of Martin Luther King, Jr.* (Valley Forge: Judson Press, 1974), 119–40.

3. Walter Brueggemann, *Living Toward a Vision: Biblical Reflections on Shalom* (Cleveland: United Church Press, 1976), 20.

4. See Paul W. Chilcote, *A Faith That Sings: Biblical Themes in the Lyrical Theology of Charles Wesley* (Eugene, OR: Cascade Books, 2017), 106–21 (Chapter 8: Dominion: Situated in God's Shalom). Many of the insights presented here depend greatly upon this earlier work.

5. Charles Wesley, *Hymns for the Nativity of our Lord*, 23–24.

in heaven, but a state to be enjoyed on earth."[6] He yearned earnestly for the inbreaking of God's rule in the here and now.

Given the fact that Jesus' life and ministry revolved around the kingdom of God more than anything else, it should be no surprise that it figures prominently as a theme in John Wesley's standard sermons. One of the most important sermons in this regard is "The Way to the Kingdom," based on Mark 1:15.[7] In this sermon he defines "true religion" as living in God's reign. Authentic discipleship consists of righteousness, peace, and joy in the Holy Spirit. It is about loving God as fully as possible and loving your neighbor as yourself. Such a love, he argues, fulfills all laws. It is the totality of what it means to be a Christian. If you root your life in God's rule, then peace and joy and love will fill your hearts. He makes it absolutely clear that this is the goal of living in the Wesleyan way.

In this final conversation, therefore, we explore true religion—the quiet and peaceable reign of Christ.[8] This is really the whole point of this book. We want to talk with you about what it means for you to align yourself with God's reign and rule as an authentic disciple of Jesus Christ. Many of you pray daily for God's kingdom to come in the Lord's Prayer (Matt 6:10). What does this mean? How do we live into this? To answer these questions, we need to explore several key elements in the Wesleys' conception of the peaceable reign of Christ: the gift of reconciliation; Christ's dominion in the human heart; the fruits of peace, joy, and righteousness; and our partnership with God in God's mission of love in and for the world.

First, *reconciliation is the foundation of the peaceable reign*. As in his doctrine of redemption (see Conversation 6), the concepts of reconciliation and restoration (see Conversation 8) play a central role in his

6. Wesley, *New Testament Notes*, comment on Matt 3:2.

7. Wesley, *Works*, 1:217–32. This was one of Wesley's favorite texts. In the 48-year span between 1742 and 1790, he preached on this text no less than 190 times (see p. 217).

8. The Wesleys build this concept of God's reign upon the foundation of the Hebrew Scriptures. The following pertinent texts figure prominently: Leviticus 26:3-6, Psalm 85:10, Hosea 2:18-20 and 32:17-18, and Isaiah 11:6-9.

concept of God's reign and rule. In the Wesleys' view, we do not build the kingdom; rather, God must restore the rule of Christ, and this entails reconciliation.

"God was in Christ, reconciling the world unto himself," St. Paul reminds the Corinthian church, "not imputing their trespasses unto them; and hath committed unto us the word of reconciliation" (2 Cor 5:19 KJV). In summary statements like this one, Paul captures God's entire mission. Friendship, even intimacy, with God characterizes this vision of life. Those drawn into this realm love both God and neighbor. Christ makes this kind of existence possible by breaking down all the barriers that divide people and disrupt God's intended harmony throughout creation.

Reconciliation itself is both the foundation and the sign of God's peaceable reign and the nearness of God's rule. Your reconciliation with God in Christ is an accomplished fact. But the reconciliation of the cosmos is a continuing process into which you and the whole community of faith are invited. We partner with God in this great work of reconciliation and restoration. God calls us to represent God's alternative vision in the world. We are called to stand in the juncture, as it were, between the old world that is passing away and the new world—the peaceable reign—that is being birthed in Christ, despite all appearances to the contrary.

Charles Wesley describes this true foundation of the peaceable reign as the "reconciling word":

> See me, Saviour, from above,
> Nor suffer me to die!
> Life, and happiness, and love,
> Drop from thy gracious eye;
> Speak the reconciling word,
> And let thy mercy melt me down;
> Turn, and look upon me, Lord,
> And break my heart of stone.[9]

Second, *the peaceable reign resides in the heart*. For the Wesleys, as

9. Wesley, *Hymns and Sacred Poems* (1749), 1:122.

we have seen, everything begins with the heart. In his reflections on Luke 17:21, John Wesley observes:

> For behold the kingdom of God is within or among you—look not for it in distant times or remote places: it is now in the midst of you: it is come: it is present in the soul of every believer: it is a spiritual kingdom, an internal principle. Wherever it exists, it exists in the heart.[10]

Charles Wesley expresses his longing for God's dominion in the hearts of all people:

> When shall thy Spirit reign
> In every heart of man?
> Father, bring the kingdom near,
> Honor thy triumphant Son,
> God of heaven, on earth appear,
> Fix with us thy glorious throne.[11]

Both brothers, however, connect this interior life of the spirit intimately with the believer's engagement in "kingdom ministry." Those who turn over their hearts to God for God's use receive God's power both to do so and to live as God's children (see 1 Cor 4:20). But unlike the power of the world, this power is that of Christ's passion. In his reflections on 1 Corinthians 4:20, Charles identifies the origins and nature of the power of love in the peaceable reign:

> If Jesus doth reign, and save us from sin,
> No words can explain his kingdom within,
> No boastful reflection on what we possess,
> No talk of perfection, or flourish of grace.
>
> Wherever our Lord his Spirit imparts,
> The kingdom restored is power in our hearts,
> The power of his passion, and rising we prove,
> The strength of salvation, the virtue of love.

10. Wesley, *New Testament Notes*, comment on Luke 17:21.
11. Wesley, *Scripture Hymns*, 2:142.

With love we receive the power to obey,
Unspotted to live, unwearied to pray:
His burdens we bear, while here we remain,
His agonies share, and suffer to reign.[12]

Third, *the fruits of the peaceable reign are righteousness, joy, and peace*. Invariably, the Wesleys turn to Romans 14:17 to describe the characteristics of this rule in human hearts—the kingdom of God is righteousness, and peace, and joy. In his poetic corpus Charles defines Christ's peaceable reign along the lines of this important trilogy.

Bring in the kingdom of his peace,
Fill all our souls with joy unknown,
And stablish us in righteousness,
And perfect all his saints in one.[13]

John preaches what Charles sings:

> This is that kingdom of heaven or of God which is "within" us, even "righteousness, and peace and joy in the Holy Ghost." And what is righteousness but the life of God in the soul, the mind which was in Christ Jesus, the image of God stamped upon the heart, now renewed after the likeness of him that created it? What is it but the love of God because he first loved us, and the love of all mankind for his sake?[14]

These constitutive elements of the peaceable reign also have a critical social dimension, as alluded to above. God's dominion begins in the human heart most certainly, but extends into the church, and then expands yet further to the poor and the persecuted—the victims of injustice. "For Methodists this internal transformation was not enough," observes Andrew Winckles, "the true evidence of the kingdom of God

12. Wesley, *Hymns and Sacred Poems* (1749), 2:291.

13. John and Charles Wesley, *Collection of Moral and Sacred Poems,* 3 vols. (Bristol: Farley, 1744), 3:241. Modernized text.

14. Wesley, *Works*, 1:481.

in heart and life was in how it worked outward into community."[15] In his peaceable reign Christ inextricably binds righteousness, joy, and peace together with justice and compassion.

Fourth, *living into the peaceable reign means partnering with God in God's mission of love.* Charles Wesley composed a hymn for his wife on their wedding day. It describes the translation of heart love into loving action in and for the world. In the following stanza he alludes to the Christ we encounter through our loving actions among poor and those in need (see Matt 25:40):

> Then let us attend
> Our heavenly friend,
> In his members distressed,
> With want, or affliction, or sickness oppressed:
> The prisoner relieve,
> The stranger receive,
> Supply all their wants,
> And spend, and be spent in assisting his saints.[16]

The hymn encourages bride and groom to be accountable to one another in love and in works of mercy as a performance of God's rule in their lives.

God invites us to become partners in the realization of shalom in the world. The Wesleys believed that God designed the church as a redemptive community, a family that lives in and for this vision. This makes it an alternative community. The church draws committed Christian disciples perennially to Jesus and to one another in community and then spins them out into the world in mission and service. Their missional practice mirrored their understanding of God—the loving Creator of all who is active and at work in the world to save and restore all creation.

---

15. Andrew Winckles, "Kingdom of God—Kingdom of Man: Freedom, Identity, and Justice in Charles Wesley and William Blake," unpublished paper presented at the North American Society for the Study of Romanticism Conference, Park City, Utah, August 12, 2011, unnumbered pages.

16. Wesley, *Hymns and Sacred Poems* (1749), 2:281.

In a sermon based on Matthew 5:13-16—part of Jesus' sermon on the mount—John Wesley provides a clarion call to a faith that works by love. He connects the quest for beloved community with the pursuit of holiness in life. He preaches faith made effective through loving action in the world:

> Those of you who are Christians "are the light of the world" with regard both to your dispositions and actions. Your holiness makes you as conspicuous as the sun in the midst of heaven. As you cannot go out of the world, so neither can you stay in it without appearing to all humankind. You may not flee from any, and while you are among them it is impossible to hide your lowliness and meekness and those other dispositions whereby you aspire to be perfect, as your Father which is in heaven is perfect. Love cannot be hid any more than light, and least of all when it shines forth in action.[17]

Note how he roots his call to Christian perfection in the concrete actions of witness, mission, and service. He very seldom conceives the Christian life on a theoretical level; rather, he orients all Christian practice to this goal of perfect love. Concrete practice of love—bearing witness to the light—leads to a fuller love of God and others. There is no place for the privatization of the Christian faith in the Wesleys. Faith is neither private, nor simplistically individualistic. Faith in Christ requires concrete, visible action in community for the sake of the world.

In his hymns, Charles counts the cost of this form of discipleship. Partnering with God in God's mission of love in the world requires commitment and courage:

> If so low a child as I
> May to thy great glory live,
> All my actions sanctify,
> All my words and thoughts receive;
> Claim me for thy service, claim
> All I have and all I am.

17. Wesley, *Works*, 1:539–40.

Take my soul and body's powers,
    Take my memory, mind, and will,
All my goods, and all my hours,
    All I know, and all I feel,
All I think, and speak, and do;
Take my heart—and make it new.[18]

This "kingdom" work included acts of compassion and justice. The Wesleys believed these two works of mercy went hand in hand. Charles's hymns express the depth of compassion lived out by the early Methodists, women in particular. Here is his lyrical portrait of Mary Naylor—one of the Methodist leaders in Bristol we met in the previous conversation—just one among thousands of empathetic Methodists:

Affliction, poverty, disease,
Drew out here soul in soft distress,
    The wretched to relieve;
In all the works of love employed,
Her sympathizing soul enjoyed
    The blessedness to give.

A nursing mother to the poor,
For them she husbanded her store,
    Her life, her all, bestowed;
For them she labored day and night,
In doing good her whole delight,
    In copying after God.[19]

The Wesleys' doctrine of the peaceable reign demonstrates God's love for the poor, their important role in the community of faith, and the responsibility of all faithful disciples to engage in advocacy for all who are dispossessed. This goal is nothing less than "paradise restored,"[20] and they pray ultimately, with all creation, for the fullest possible realization of the peaceable reign of Christ in and for all.

---

18. Wesley, *Hymns on the Lord's Supper,* 129–30.
19. Charles Wesley, *Funeral Hymns*, 53.
20. Wesley, *Scripture Hymns*, 2:76.

Fifth, *the coming peaceable reign depends on the integrity of authentic Christians*. We want to offer you a postscript of sorts to this final conversation about living the Wesleyan way in and for the world. In doing so, we also want to leave you with John Wesley's own words related to authentic Christian living. In 1753, he published *A Plain Account of Genuine Christianity*. John and his brother, Charles, devoted the entirety of their lives to the recovery of this very thing.

Then, as in our own day, many people had little idea of what an authentic Christian looked like. Today, whether distorted by misrepresentations in the media or bad examples within the ranks of the church itself, many people quite simply associate Christianity with hypocrisy and judgmentalism. Tragically, Christians themselves are often the greatest obstacle to God for other people. John Wesley, therefore, wanted to be very clear about Christian authenticity. He provides this portrait of the genuine Christian, filled with love and motivated by mercy and grace.

Note the wide embrace of the genuine Christian. Love knows no bounds. In the same way that God's love reaches out to every human being, so the love of the authentic disciple of Jesus "ingrasps all humankind," to use the language of Charles Wesley. Genuine love is not simply a feeling or an attitude. Wesley makes it clear that love must be translated in action, and that this action must be consistent with the love toward which it seeks to point. Genuine love expressed by authentic Christians leads to genuine reconciliation, fellowship, and mutual love. This is the legacy we inherit from John and Charles Wesley. We commend this vision of living the Wesleyan way to you. It is a vision in and for the world that God so desperately loves. So let's give John and Charles Wesley the final word here. We leave you with two excerpts from the writings of John and a hymn from the pen of Charles.

> Remembering that God is love, genuine Christians are conformed to the same likeness. They are full of love for their neighbors, of universal love, not confined to one sect or party, not restrained to those who agree with them in opinions or in outward modes of worship or to those who are allied to them by blood or recommended by nearness

> of place. Neither do they love those only that love them or that are endeared to them by intimacy of acquaintance. But their love resembles that of God whose mercy is over all God's works. It soars above all these scanty bounds, embracing neighbors and strangers, friends and enemies, yes, not only the good and gentle but also the disobedient, the evil and unthankful. For they love every soul that God has made, every child of humanity.[21]
>
> Let love not visit you as a transient guest, but be the constant ruling disposition of your soul. See that your heart is filled at all times and on all occasions with real, genuine benevolence, not to those only that love you, but to every soul. Let it pant in your heart, let it sparkle in your eyes, let it shine on all your actions. Whenever you open your lips, let it be with love, and let the law of kindness be on your tongue. Your word will then distill as the rain and as the dew upon the tender herb. Be not constrained or limited in your affection, but let it embrace every child of God. Everyone that is born of a woman has a claim to your goodwill. You owe this not to some, but to all. And let all people know that you desire both their temporal and eternal happiness as sincerely as you do your own.[22]

All these words celebrate love. Love is the beginning, the journey, and the goal. Moving upward in Wesleyan formation, more than anything else, means living into the quiet and peaceable reign of Christ in and for the world. Come, Lord Jesus; come quickly and establish your rule of love in every heart.

> Come, thou holy God and true!
> Come, and my whole heart renew;
> Take me now, possess me whole,
> Form the Saviour in my soul.
>
> Happy soul, whose active love
> Emulates the blest above,

---

21. John Wesley, *A Plain Account of Genuine Christianity,* in *Works* (Jackson), 10:68.

22. Wesley, *Works*, 3:422–23.

In thy every action seen,
Sparkling from the soul within.

Only feel'st within thee move
Tenderness, compassion, love,
Love immense, and unconfin'd,
Love to all of humankind.

Love, which willeth all should live,
Love, which all to all would give,
Love, that over all prevails,
Love, that never, never fails.[23]

23. Wesley, *Hymns and Sacred Poems* (1749), 1:38–39.

Reflection Questions

Conversation 12 (Peaceable Reign)

1. What part of this Conversation spoke most to you? Why is it important for you to hear this right now?

2. In what areas of your life has it been easy to cultivate a "heart of peace," and where have you struggled? Where are the struggles?

3. As you reflect on this upward journey, what do you carry away from these conversations into your daily life?

Beginning: The Fourth Movement of the Way

We have engaged in a lot of conversation together. In John Wesley's manuscript diary, the notation that occurred more frequently than any other was a cypher easily transcribed to two letters: "rt." This meant "religious talk." So much of his life was invested in serious conversation with all different kinds of men, women, and children. And most of those conversations were about God, about life, and about love. In his mind, however, that talk had to be translated into action. We want our final words with you to be about translating all these conversations—all this talk—into action. We are calling this Movement 4. Most books end with a Conclusion; we want our book to end with a Beginning. This is where it all starts, really.

In the first two Movements we emphasized words that have to do with the character of a Methodist and the Wesleyan way. This way shaped by deep wisdom elevates grace, humility, inclusivity, and love. These have to do with your spirit—those internal qualities that define your soul. We also live upward in Wesleyan formation with wonder. Words like grandeur, dignity, delight, and glory express our wonder as we contemplate all God has done for us through acts of creation, redemption, sustenance, and restoration. The verbs of Movement 3 begin that translation of these ideas in actions. Living in and for the world involves gospel-bearing, forming, honoring, and living into God's reign.

We pray that, when others encounter the people called Methodists, they will see and experience followers of Jesus who exhibit these qualities. We pray that all our being and our doing resembles Christ. We seek to be like him in every way. To be true to the Wesleys, you must not only talk about the gospel, you must be the gospel for others. We pray that you have the courage to pick up the mantel of a mystic-prophet in the same way that Elisha embraced this challenge from Elijah (1 Kings 19). Our deep desire is for you to honor the unity of all things and the integrity of God's holistic vision and purposes. Finally, and perhaps most importantly, we yearn for you to love and to create communities that are known for their love in the world.

We have spent decades as Wesleyan scholars seeking to live the Wesleyan way that we have described and commended in this book. We believe that the purpose of theology is to form us into Christlikeness. We take our cue from Jesus, who said he came that we might live abundantly (John 10:10). We see the Wesleys as seekers after this abundance all their days, and over the course of more than half a century "offering Christ" to all in many ways. We have written about the wisdom, wonder, and work of their mission, and even though we have provided details in this book, we have left much unsaid. You will write the Fourth Movement of this book by living the Wesleyan way. In this "beginning," therefore, we want to step away from the particulars and offer a pattern for living the Wesleyan way—a template that can be used to find and follow that way.

We want this way of "living in Christ" to be concrete and practical. The template we recommend to you has three components that align with the movements of this book. The Wesleyan means of grace frame the template in a life apprenticed to Christ—a disciple's life drawn to Christ and spun out into the world in loving service. Think of this as a "rule of life" in the Wesleyan way.

First, *living by Christ*. We invite you to practice the wisdom of the Wesleyan way by engaging in two particular works of piety: prayer and immersion in scripture. These practices cultivate humility and love in heart and life. Dedicate time each day to be with God in prayer and to read and ponder God's Word. Consider beginning and/or ending each day with a form of Morning Prayer and Evening Prayer. *The United Methodist Hymnal* provides a simple pattern for both these practices (pp. 876–79) that engage prayer and scripture.

Second, *living with Christ.* We invite you to live in wonder each day. Practice the presence of God, as Brother Lawrence would say. In our experience, two additional Wesleyan works of piety open our hearts and lives to the wonder that surrounds us at all times: Christian fellowship and Eucharist. Living with Christ is a shared adventure. These practices have stood the test of time in terms of their ability to restore the soul. Join a small group. Avail yourself of Holy Communion whenever it is celebrated. Engage in these practices as often as you can. We recommend at least once a week.

Third, living *in and for* Christ. We invite you to engage in Wesleyan works of mercy as well: compassion and justice. Living in and for Christ means to live in and for the world that God loves. You will find people around you each day who are lonely, wounded, and in great need. Each week find a way to "be love" to someone. Practice compassion by offering a listening ear, a healing hug, words of comfort and genuine caring. Injustice abounds in our world; you need not go far to find it. Open your eyes to injustice in your neighborhood or immediate community. What can you do to right the wrongs you perceive? Engage with others in conversation about how you can be a solution to problems and a presence of reconciliation. Engage in these works of mercy as God presents opportunity.

Living by Christ—prayer and scripture
Living with Christ—Christian fellowship and Eucharist
Living in and for Christ—compassion and justice

The early Methodist people practiced these works of piety and works of mercy. Small groups shaped their life of faith and provided the accountability they needed to grow in grace and love. We believe that this three-fold template provides a means to grow in Christ—by and with Christ in and for the sake of the world. In our experience, more than anything else, joy and gratitude characterize this life.

One of the first things John Wesley published was an abridgement of Thomas á Kempis' *The Imitation of Christ*. He entitled it, *The Christian's Pattern*. He saw in this devotional classic the main ingredients for living the Christian life, and he wanted others to embrace that pattern as well. We offer to you our own Christian's pattern, therefore, one that is Christological in spirit and substance.

We begin by offering Christ in his person, as the Word made flesh. He is our incarnate example. If the Word had remained Word, we might conclude that abundant living is unattainable, at least not fully in this life. Our faith would be admirable, but it would be abstract. The Incarnation changes all that, moving eternity into time—the "there and later" into the "here and now."

We are glad to see the term "Human One" being used for the incarnate Christ. It makes clear in an inclusive sense that whatever else the Christian life is, it is realistic. Jesus lived the life God intends for all to live. We cannot defer that life to a future time or deflect it as a life for others but not us. Jesus lived the abundant life, and so can we. The person of Jesus not only puts a face on God, he also puts one on us.

We also offer Christ in his *work*. We can speak of this in terms akin to some of the names he is given, like prophet, priest, and king. We note that Jesus applied all this—his prophetic, priestly, and royal work—to "the least of these," and told us to do the same. He incarnated God's concern for the *anawim,* those without a voice, who were routinely ignored, stigmatized, marginalized, and oppressed. Jesus challenged the fallen-world system, disobeying some of its unjust laws, and proactively showing compassion to those left to fend for themselves. He "saw" and cared for those who had become invisible and expendable.

We are glad that the social-justice dimension of Jesus is being recovered and emphasized today. Richard Foster sees this in the compassionate life of Jesus. He incarnated three great emphases in the Hebrew scriptures: *mishpat* (equitable distribution), *hesed* (loving kindness), and *shalom* (comprehensive wellbeing).[1] We see and celebrate the resurgence of nonviolent resistance to evil through the practice of love.[2]

From the person and work of Jesus (the incarnate Christ) we move to offer the "excarnate Christ" in his presence and glory. With respect to presence, we claim his promise: "And remember, I am with you always, to the end of the age" (Matt 28:20). We simply emphasize that the risen Christ is with us, dwelling in our hearts, conforming our minds to his own, and working through our hands. With respect to his glory we acknowledge the upside down way in which God works. The early Christian hymn that St. Paul quotes in his letter to the Philippians (2:5-11), as we have seen, figured prominently in the theology of the Wesleys. We have emphasized the first part of that hymn throughout these conversations because it reminds us about Jesus' posture of humility. But a "therefore" stands as a critical transition in the center of that hymn about the servant-savior:

> Therefore God exalted him even more highly and gave him the name that is above every other name, so that at the name given to Jesus every knee should bend, in heaven and on earth and under the earth, and every tongue should confess that Jesus Christ is Lord, to the glory of God the Father. (2:9-11)

We are living in a time when many are rediscovering the universal Christ. We are extremely happy about this and have written about this earlier in the book in the movement on wonder. We can never overestimate the importance of the glory of Christ in time and in

---

1. Richard Foster, *Streams of Living Water* (New York: HarperOne, 1998), 166–72.

2. We highlight this through the ministries of John Dear, William Barber III, Jonathan Wilson-Hartgrove, Lisa Sharon Harper, and Steven Charleston—to name a few—and with abiding appreciation for Dorothy Day, Howard Thurman, Martin Luther King, Jr., and Jose Hobday—again, to name a few. In the Wesleyan tradition we give thanks for the witness of Georgia Harkness, Nelson Mandela, James Lawson, and Peter Storey.

eternity. We dare not miss this treasure. We live with eyes wide open so as never to miss it. We believe it is the Wesleyan way to live beyond our preferences to discover all the ways the Lord of Glory is known, loved, and served by the human family in the world today.

Putting it all together, then, we live the Wesleyan way by living by Christ, with Christ, and in and for Christ. Christ is our life (Rom 6:23) and our hope (1 Tim 1:1). Living the upward adventure means reflecting his person and manifesting his work, through the grace given to us by God. Through all the days of our lives, we confirm the truth of John Wesley's final words, "The best of all is, God is with us." Emmanuel. With lives built upon this firm foundation, we offer ourselves to God as living sacrifices (Rom 12:1), as instruments of God's peace, moving into the world in Jesus' name.

Paul's book, *Active Faith,* ends with a mandate to translate faith into action. We offer it again here, staking our claim that these words capture the essence of living the Wesleyan way. We invite you to make your own commitment to living this way as you read these words:

> With confidence in the promises of God,
> faith in Jesus Christ,
> and in the power of the Holy Spirit,
> we declare:

We find Truth in Jesus.

> Being found in human form,
> he emptied himself of all but love.
> Like him, we seek to lift people up,
> assuming a posture of servanthood among all.
> We pray that our practice of humility
> helps us to break down barriers of human hostility

We find Joy in Jesus.

> He made room for others
> and invited all people into the sacred space of love.
> Like him, we seek to create safe spaces for others,
> turning enemies into friends.

We pray that our practice of hospitality
helps build bridges and tear down walls.

We find Peace in Jesus.

He embraced a mission of love,
caring for all and restoring God's world.
Like him, we seek to partner with God
in the recovery of God's vision of shalom.
We pray that our practice of healing
helps us to restore peace with justice everywhere.

We find Love in Jesus.

He demonstrated the fullest possible extent
of the love of God and neighbor.
Like him, we seek to live a life of faith
working by love leading to holiness.
We pray that our practice of holiness
helps others to discover their true identity
as the beloved children of God.

We embrace the holistic and all-inclusive vision
of God's restoration of beloved community.[3]

3. Chilcote, *Active Faith*, 75–76.

– Bibliography –

Books, Chapters, and Articles

Albin, Tom. "Finding God in Small Groups." *Christianity Today* 47, 8 (August 2003): 42–44.

Baker, Frank. *John Wesley and the Church of England.* Nashville: Abingdon Press, 1970.

Bebbington, David. *Evangelicalism in Modern Britain: A History from the 1730s to the 1980s.* Grand Rapids: Baker Book House, 1989.

Berry, Thomas. *The Sacred Universe: Earth, Spirituality, and Religion in the Twenty-first Century.* New York: Columbia University Press, 2009.

Bonhoeffer, Dietrich. *Letter and Papers from Prison.* New York: Touchstone, 1997.

Bourgeault, Cynthia. *The Heart of Centering Prayer: Nondual Christianity in Theory and Practice.* Boston: Shambhala, 2016.

———. *The Wisdom Jesus: Transforming Heart and Mind—A New Perspective on Christ and His Message.* Boston: Shambhala, 2008.

Bouteneff, Peter. "All Creation in United Thanksgiving: Gregory of Nyssa and the Wesleys on Salvation" In *Orthodox and Wesleyan Spirituality.* Edited by S T Kimbrough, Jr., 187–99. Crestwood, NY: St. Vladimir's Seminary Press, 2002.

Brueggemann, Walter. *God, Neighbor, Empire: The Excess of Divine Fidelity and the Command of Common Good.* Waco, TX: Baylor University Press, 2016.

———. *Living Toward a Vision: Biblical Reflections on Shalom.* Cleveland: United Church Press, 1976.

———. *The Prophetic Imagination.* Revised edition. Minneapolis, Fortress Press, 2001.

———. *Reality, Grief, Hope: Three Urgent Prophetic Tasks.* Grand Rapids: William B. Eerdmans, 2014.

———. *Spirituality of the Psalms.* Minneapolis: Fortress Press, 2001.

Campbell, Ted A. *The Religion of the Heart.* Eugene, OR: Wipf & Stock, 2000.

Chilcote, Paul W. *Active Faith: Resisting 4 Dangerous Ideologies with the Wesleyan Way.* Nashville: Abingdon Press, 2019.

———. "'All the Image of Thy Love': Charles Wesley's Vision of the One Thing Needful." *Proceedings of The Charles Wesley Society* 18 (2014): 21–40.

———. "Charles Wesley and the Peaceable Reign of Christ." *Holiness: An International Journal of Wesleyan Theology*, forthcoming.

———. "Eucharist and Formation." In *Theology, Eucharist and Ministry: Wesleyan Perspectives.* Edited by Jason E. Vickers, 183–201. Nashville: General Board of Higher Education and Ministry, 2016.

———. *A Faith That Sings: Biblical Themes in the Lyrical Theology of Charles Wesley.* Eugene, OR: Cascade Books, 2016.

———. *The Imitation of Christ: Selections Annotated & Explained.* Woodstock, VT: SkyLight Paths, 2012.

———. "John and Charles Wesley on 'God in Christ Reconciling.'" *Methodist History* 47, 3 (April 2009), 132–45.

———. *"'Practical Christology' in John and Charles Wesley." In Methodist Christology: From the Wesleys to the Twenty-First Century.* Edited by Jason Vickers, 3–35. Nashville: Wesley Foundery Books, 2020.

———. *The Quest for Love Divine: Select Essays in Wesleyan Theology and Practice.* Eugene, OR: Cascade Books, 2022.

———. *Recapturing the Wesleys' Vision: An Introduction to the Faith of John and Charles Wesley.* Downers Grove, IL: InterVarsity Press, 2004.

———. *Singing the Faith: Soundings of Lyrical Theology in the Methodist Tradition.* Nashville: Wesley's Foundery Books, 2020.

———. ed. *The Wesleyan Tradition: A Paradigm for Renewal.* Nashville: Abingdon Press, 2002.

Chilcote, Paul W., and Steve Harper. *A Living Hope: An Inclusive Vision of the Future.* Eugene: Cascade Books, 2019.

Clapper, Gregory S. *As if the Heart Mattered.* Nashville: Upper Room Books, 1997.

———. *The Renewal of the Heart in the Mission of the Church.* Eugene: Cascade Books, 2010.

Christiansen, Michael J. "The Royal Way of Love: Deification in the Wesleyan Tradition." In *With All the Fullness of God.* Edited by Jared Ortiz, 177–202. London: Lexington Books, 2021.

Church, Leslie F. *More About the Early Methodist People.* London: Epworth Press, 1949.

Clarke, Adam. *Memoirs of the Late Eminent Mrs. Mary Cooper, of London.* New edition. Halifax: William Nicholson and Sons, post-1822.

Clifford, Richard. *The Wisdom Literature.* Nashville: Abingdon Press, 1998.

Cole, Joseph, ed. *Memorials of Hannah Ball*, 3rd edition. London: Wesleyan Conference Office, 1880.

de Chardin, Pierre Teilhard. *The Divine Milieu.* New York: Harper & Row, 1960.

Delio, Ilia. *The Hours of the Universe: Reflections on God, Science, and the Human Journey.* Maryknoll, NY: Orbis Books, 2021.

deVega, Magrey R. *One Faithful Promise: The Wesleyan Covenant for Renewal.* Nashville: Abingdon Press, 2016.

Foster, Richard. *Streams of Living Water.* New York: HarperOne, 1998.

Fowler, James W. "John Wesley's Development in Faith," unpublished and undated article.

———. *Stages of Faith: The Psychology of Human Development and the Quest for Meaning.* New York: HarperCollins, 1981.

Fox, Matthew. *On Becoming a Musical, Mystical Bear.* Mahwah: Paulist Press, 1972.

———. *Original Blessing: A Primer in Creation Spirituality.* Revised edition. New York: J. P. Tarcher/Penguin, 2000.

———. *Prayer, a Radical Response to Life.* New York: Tarcher, 2001.

Harper, Steve. *Devotional Life in the Wesleyan Tradition: A Workbook.* Nashville: Upper Room Books, 1995.

———. *Five Marks of a Methodist.* Nashville: Abingdon Press, 2015.

———. *Holy Love: A Biblical Theology of Human Sexuality.* Nashville: Abingdon Press, 2019.

———. "John Wesley: Spiritual Guide." *Wesleyan Theological Journal* 20, 2 (Fall 1985): 93–98.

———. *The Way to Heaven: The Gospel according to John Wesley.* Grand Rapids: Zondervan, 2003.

———. "Wesley's Sermons as Spiritual Formation Documents." *Methodist History* 26 (April 1988): 131–38.

Heath, Elaine. *Five Means of Grace: Experience God's Love the Wesleyan Way.* Nashville: Abingdon Press, 2017.

———. *The Mystic Way of Evangelism.* Grand Rapids: Baker Academic, 2008.

Hinton, David. *Wild Mind, Wild Earth.* Boston: Shambhala, 2022.

Hunsberger, George. "Everything You've Wanted to Know about *Missional* (But Didn't Know to Ask) An interview with George Hunsberger." *ReNews.*

Jennings, Theodore Jr. *Good News to the Poor.* Nashville: Abingdon Press, 1990.

Jones, E. Stanley. *The Divine Yes.* Nashville: Abingdon Press, 1975.

———. *In Christ.* Nashville: Abingdon Press, 1961.

———. *The Unshakable Kingdom and the Unchanging Person.* Nashville: Abingdon Press, 1972.

———. *The Way.* Nashville: Abingdon Press, 1946.

Jorgenson, Kiara A., and Alan G. Padgett, eds. *Ecotheology: A Christian Conversation.* Grand Rapids: Wm. B. Eerdmans, 2020.

Kimbrough, S T Jr. "Charles Wesley and the Journey of Sanctification." *Evangelical Journal* 16 (1998): 49–75.

———. *A Heart to Praise My God.* Nashville: Abingdon Press, 2000.

———. *The Lyrical Theology of Charles Wesley: A Reader.* Eugene, OR: Wipf & Stock, 2011.

———, ed. *Evangelization, the Heart of Mission: A Wesleyan Imperative.* New York: General Board of Global Ministries, 1995.

Kimbrough, S T Jr. and Kenneth G. C. Newport *The Manuscript Journal of the Reverend Charles Wesley, M.A.* 2 volumes. Nashville: Kingswood Books, 2007.

Kinlaw, Dennis F. *The Mind of Christ.* Grand Rapids: Francis Asbury Press, 1998.

Knight, Henry H., III. *The Presence of God in the Christian Life: John Wesley and the Means of Grace.* Metuchen, NJ: Scarecrow Press, 1992.

Lopez, Shane, Jennifer Teramoto Pedrotti, and C. R. Snyder. *Positive Psychology: The Scientific and Practical Explorations of Human Strengths.* Los Angeles: Sage Publications, 2019.

Luther, Martin. *Luther's Works, Volume 36, Word and Sacrament II.* Edited by Abdel R. Wentz. Minneapolis: Augsburg Fortress Pub., 1959.

Maddox, Randy L. "'Anticipate Our Heaven Below': The Emphatic Hope and Abiding Tone of Charles Wesley's Eschatology." *Proceedings of the Charles Wesley Society* 17 (2013): 11–34.

———. "John Wesley and Eastern Orthodoxy: Influences, Convergences, and Differences." *Asbury Theological Journal* 45, 2 (1990): 29–53.

———. *Responsible Grace: John Wesley's Practical Theology.* Nashville: Kingswood Books, 1994.

———. "Salvation as Flourishing for the Whole Creation: A Wesleyan Trajectory." In *Wesleyan Perspectives on Human Flourishing.* Edited by Dean G. Smith and Rob A. Fringer, 1–23. Eugene, OR: Pickwick, 2021

Mayo, Harold. *John Wesley and the Christian East: On the Subject of Christian Perfection.* Crestwood, NY: St. Vladimir's Orthodox Theological Seminary, 1980.

Meistad, Tore. "The Missiology of Charles Wesley and Its Links to the Eastern Church." In *Orthodox and Wesleyan Spirituality.* Edited by S T Kimbrough Jr., 205–31. Crestwood, NY: St. Vladimir's Seminary Press, 2002.

Mercer, Jerry L. *Living Deeply Our New Life in Christ.* Nashville: Discipleship Resources, 1999.

Moltmann, Jürgen. *Theology of Hope.* Minneapolis: Fortress Press, 1993.

Newell, John Philip. *Listening for the Heartbeat of God: A Celtic Spirituality.* Mahwah: Paulist Press, 1997.

———. *One Foot in Eden: A Celtic View of the Stages of Life.* Mahweh, NJ: Paulist Press, 1999.

———. *The Rebirthing of God: Christianity's Struggle for New Beginnings.* Woodstock, VT: Skylight Paths, 2015.

Nouwen, Henri. *Life of the Beloved.* New York: Crossroad, 1992.

———. *Reaching Out: The Three Movements of the Spiritual Life.* New York: Image Books, 1986.

Oord, Thomas Jay. *Pluriform Love: An Open and Relational Theology of Well-being*. Grasmere, ID: SacraSage Press, 2022.

Outler, Albert C. *Evangelism in the Wesleyan Spirit*. Nashville: Tidings, 1971.

———. *Theology in the Wesleyan Spirit*. Nashville: Tidings Press, 1975.

Palmer, Parker. *A Hidden Wholeness*. San Francisco: Josey Bass, 2004.

Peterson, Eugene. *Christ Plays in Ten Thousand Places*. Grand Rapids: Eerdmans, 2005.

———. *A Long Obedience in the Same Direction: Discipleship in an Instant Society*. Downers Grove, IL: InterVarsity Press, 1980.

Pinnock, Clark K., and Robert C. Brow. *Unbounded Love: A Good News Theology for the 21st Century*. Eugene, OR; Wipf & Stock, 2000.

Pohl, Christine D. *Making Room: Recovering Hospitality as a Christian Tradition*. Grand Rapids: Wm. B. Eerdmans, 1999.

Rainey, David. "Beauty in Creation: John Wesley's Natural Philosophy." *Wesley and Methodist Studies* 9, 1 (2017): 18–35.

Rattenbury, J. Ernest. *The Evangelical Doctrines of Charles Wesley's Hymns*. London: Epworth Press, 1954.

Robert, Dana L. *Evangelism as the Heart of Mission*. New York: General Board of Global Ministries, 1997.

Robertson, Brandon J. *The Gospel of Inclusion: A Christian Case for LGBT+ Inclusion in the Church*. Revised edition. Eugene, OR: Cascade Books, 2022.

Rogers, Hester Ann. *An Account of the Experience of Hester Ann Rogers*. New York: Hunt & Eaton, 1893.

Rohr, Richard. *The Divine Dance: The Trinity and Your Transformation*. New Kensington, PA: Whitaker House, 2016.

———. *Essential Teachings on Love*. Maryknoll: Orbis Books, 2018.

———. *Everything Belongs*. Revised and expanded edition. New York: Crossroad, 2003.

———. *The Naked Now*. New York: Crossroad, 2009.

———. *The Wisdom Pattern: Order, Disorder, Reorder*. Cincinnati: Franciscan Media, 2020.

Smith, Kenneth L., and Ira G. Zepp, Jr. *Search for the Beloved Community: The Thinking of Martin Luther King, Jr.* Valley Forge: Judson Press, 1974.

Snyder, Howard. "Holistic Mission and the Wesleyan Pentalateral," unpublished paper, 2006.

Spina, Frank A. *The Faith of the Outsider: Exclusion and Inclusion in the Biblical Story*. Grand Rapids: Wm. B. Eerdmans, 2005.

Tooth, Mary Tooth. *A Letter to the Loving and Beloved People of the Parish of Madeley [by Mary Fletcher]*. Shiffnal: Printed by A. Edmonds, n.d.

Tuttle, Robert. *Mysticism in the Wesleyan Tradition*. Grand Rapids: Zondervan, 1989.

The United Methodist Book of Worship. Nashville: The United Methodist Publishing House, 1992.

The United Methodist Hymnal. Nashville: The United Methodist Publishing House, 1989.

Volf, Miroslav. *Exclusion and Embrace: A Theological Exploration of Identity, Otherness, and Reconciliation*. Revised and updated edition. Nashville: Abingdon Press, 2019.

Wainwright, Geoffrey. "Trinitarian Theology and Wesleyan Holiness." In *Orthodox and Wesleyan Spirituality*. Edited by S T Kimbrough Jr., 59–80. Yonkers, NY: St. Vladimir's Seminary Press, 2002.

Wakefield, Gordon S. *Methodist Spirituality*. London: Epworth Press, 1999.

Ware, Kallistos. *The Orthodox Way*. Revised edition. Yonkers, NY: St. Vladimir's Seminary Press, 2012.

Wesley, Charles. *Funeral Hymns*. Bristol: Farley, 1759.

———. *Hymns and Sacred Poems*. 2 volumes. Bristol: Farley, 1749.

———. *Hymns for the Use of Families*. Bristol: Pine, 1767.

———. *Hymns for Those that Seek and Those that have Redemption in the Blood of Jesus Christ*. London: Strahan, 1747.

———. *Hymns for the Nativity of our Lord*. London: Strahan, 1745.

———. MS Acts.

———. MS Funeral Hymns.

———. *Short Hymns on Select Passages of the Holy Scriptures*. 2 volumes. Bristol: Farley, 1762.

Wesley, John. *Explanatory Notes upon the New Testament*. Bristol: William Pine, 1765.

———. *Explanatory Notes upon the Old Testament*. Bristol: William Pine, 1765.

———. *An Extract of the Life of Monsieur de Renty: A Late Nobleman of France*. Bristol: Grabham & Pine, 1760.

———. *Free Grace*. Bristol: Farley, 1739.

———. *The Letters of the Rev. John Wesley, A.M.* 8 volumes. Edited by John Telford. London: Epworth Press, 1931.

———. *A Plain Account of Christian Perfection*. Edited by Paul W. Chilcote and Randy L. Maddox. Kansas City: Beacon Hill Press, 2015.

———. *A survey of the wisdom of God in the creation: or a compendium of natural philosophy*. 2 volumes. Bristol: William Pine, 1763.

———. *The Works of John Wesley, Volume 1, Sermons I (1-33)*. Edited by Albert C. Outler. Nashville: Abingdon Press, 1984.

———. *The Works of John Wesley, Volume 2, Sermons II (34-70)*. Edited by Albert C. Outler. Nashville: Abingdon Press, 1985.

———. *The Works of John Wesley, Volume 3, Sermons III (71-114).* Edited by Albert C. Outler. Nashville: Abingdon Press, 1986.

———. *The Works of John Wesley, Volume 4, Sermons IV (115-151).* Edited by Albert C. Outler. Nashville: Abingdon Press, 1987.

———. *The Works of John Wesley, Volume 7, A Collection of Hymns for the use of the People called Methodists.* Edited by Franz Hildebrandt and Oliver A. Beckerlegge. Oxford: Clarendon Press, 1983.

———. *The Works of John Wesley, Volume 9, The Methodist Societies: History, Nature, and Design.* Edited by Rupert E. Davies. Nashville: Abingdon Press, 1989.

———. *The Works of John Wesley, Volume 10, The Methodist Societies.* Edited by Henry D. Rack. Nashville: Abingdon Press, 2011.

———. *The Works of John Wesley, Volume 13, Doctrinal and Controversial Treatises II.* Edited by Paul W. Chilcote and Kenneth J. Collins. Nashville: Abingdon Press, 2013.

———. *The Works of John Wesley, Volume 18, Journals and Diaries I (1735–1738).* Edited by W. Reginald Ward and Richard P. Heitzenrater. Nashville: Abingdon Press, 1988.

———. *The Works of John Wesley, Volume 21, Journal and Diaries IV (1755–1765).* Edited by W. Reginald Ward and Richard P. Heitzenrater. Nashville: Abingdon Press, 1992.

———. *The Works of John Wesley, Volume 27, Letters III, 1756–1765.* Edited by Ted A. Campbell. Nashville: Abingdon Press, 2015.

———. *The Works of the Rev. John Wesley, A.M.* Edited by Thomas Jackson. 14 volumes. Reprint edition. Grand Rapids: Zondervan, 1958.

Wesley, John, and Charles Wesley. *Collection of Moral and Sacred Poems.* 3 volumes. Bristol: Farley, 1744.

———. *Hymns of Petition and Thanksgiving for the Promise of Father.* Bristol: Farley, 1746.———. *Hymns and Sacred Poems.* Bristol: Farley, 1739.

———. *Hymns and Sacred Poems.* London: Strahan, 1740.

———. *Hymns and Sacred Poems.* Bristol: Farley, 1742.

———. *Hymns on the Lord's Supper.* Bristol: Farley, 1745.

Willard, Dallas. *The Divine Conspiracy: Rediscovering Our Hidden Life in God.* New York: HarperCollins, 1998.

Williams, Colin W. *John Wesley's Theology Today.* Nashville: Abingdon Press, 1960.

Wilson, Robert L., and Steve Harper. *Faith and Form: A Unity of Theology and Polity in the United Methodist Tradition.* Grand Rapids: Zondervan, 1988.

Winckles, Andrew. "Kingdom of God—Kingdom of Man: Freedom, Identity, and Justice in Charles Wesley and William Blake." Unpublished paper presented at the North American Society for the Study of Romanticism Conference, Park City, Utah, August 12, 2011. Unnumbered pages.

Wynkoop, Mildred Bangs. *A Theology of Love: The Dynamic of Wesleyanism.* 2nd edition. Kansas City: Beacon Hill, 2015.

Digital Resources

"Awaken Modern Mystics and Prophets." The Shift Network; https://theshiftnetwork.com/ModernMysticsProphets; accessed January 22, 2023.

Bell, Ian. "Writing a Rule of Life." Exploring Devotion. The Methodist Church. https://www.methodist.org.uk/media/5035/dd-explore-devotion-writing-a-rule-of-life-0313.pdf; accessed December 26, 2022.

"Covenant Renewal Service." Discipleship Ministries. The United Methodist Church; https://www.umcdiscipleship.org/resources/covenant-renewal-service; accessed January 22, 2023.

Foster, Richard. "The Six Streams: A Balanced Vision. Renovaré Institute"; https://renovare.org/about/ideas/the-six-streams; accessed January 22, 2023.

Harper, Steve. "At the Gate: Imagineers." *Oboedire* blogpost. January 2, 2023; https://oboedire.wordpress.com/2023/01/02/at-the-gate-imagineers/; accessed January 22, 2023.

"Interview of Julie Allen." Inclusion Dialogue. Joanne Banks. https://audioboom.com/posts/7734420-interview-with-professor-julie-allan; accessed December 23, 2022.

King, Coretta Scott. Facebook post, July 12, 2019; https://www.facebook.com/corettascottking/posts/to-me-the-beloved-community-is-a-realistic-vison-of-an-achievable-society-one-i/689076578230095/; accessed January 10, 2023.

"The Most Beautiful Science of the Year." Nautilus Institute. December 28, 2022; https://nautil.us/the-most-beautiful-science-of-the-year-254943/; accessed January 24, 2023.

Olson, Mark K. "From the Beginning to the End: John Wesley's Doctrine of Creation." wesleyscholar.com. March 1, 2031. https://wesleyscholar.com/from-the-beginning-to-the-end-john-wesleys-doctrine-of-creation/; accessed January 16, 2023.

Overheard Podcast. Episode 1: Resurrecting Notre-Dame de Paris, January 18, 2022; https://www.nationalgeographic.com/podcasts/article/resurrecting-notre-dame-de-paris; accessed January 20, 2023.

Snyder, Howard. "Wesley the Environmentalist?" *Catalyst*. February 1, 2009; https://www.catalystresources.org/wesley-the-environmentalist/; accessed January 24, 2023.

Printed in the USA
CPSIA information can be obtained
at www.ICGtesting.com
LVHW030838181123
763967LV00005B/7

9 781791 033071